Risk Management
for IT Projects

How to Deal with Over
150 Issues and Risks

Risk Management for IT Projects

How to Deal with Over 150 Issues and Risks

Bennet P. Lientz

Professor
Anderson Graduate School of Management
University of California, Los Angeles

Lee Larssen

President
The Strategic Edge

ELSEVIER

Amsterdam • Boston • Heidelberg • London
New York • Oxford • Paris • San Diego
San Francisco • Singapore • Sydney • Tokyo
Butterworth-Heinemann is an imprint of Elsevier

Butterworth–Heinemann is an imprint of Elsevier
30 Corporate Drive, Suite 400, Burlington, MA 01803, USA
Linacre House, Jordan Hill, Oxford OX2 8DP, UK

 Recognizing the importance of preserving what has been written, Elsevier prints its books on
acid-free paper whenever possible.

Library of Congress Cataloging-in-Publication Data
Lientz, Bennet P.
    Risk management for IT projects : how to deal with over 150 issues and risks / Bennet
P. Lientz, Lee Larssen.
        p. cm.
    Includes bibliographical references and index.
    ISBN 0-7506-8231-0 (alk. paper)
        1. Information technology—Management.   2. Risk management.   I. Larssen, Lee.
    II. Title.

HD30.2.L544 2006
004.168′1—dc22

                                                                                2006040906

British Library Cataloguing-in-Publication Data
A catalogue record for this book is available from the British Library.

ISBN 13: 978-0-7506-8231-2
ISBN 10: 0-7506-8231-0

For information on all Butterworth–Heinemann publications
visit our Web site at www.books.elsevier.com

Printed in the United States of America
06 07 08 09 10   10 9 8 7 6 5 4 3 2 1

Contents

Preface   xv

Part I

Issues and Risk Management

Chapter 1

Introduction

Effective Issues Management and Coordination

Analysis and Measurements of Issues and Risk

Part II
Internal Issues and Risk

Chapter 4
Teams

Chapter 5
The Work

Chapter 6

Business Units

Chapter 7

Management

Chapter 8

Projects

Chapter 9

Resistance to Change

Part III
External Issues and Risks

Chapter 10

Vendors, Consultants, and Outsourcing

Chapter 11

Headquarters

Chapter 12

Technology

Preface

The rate of failure of IT (information technology) projects has changed little in survey after survey over the past 15–20 years — approximately 40–50%. This has happened in spite of new technology, innovative methods and tools, and different management methods. Why does this happen? Why can't the situation be better? One reason is that many think of each IT effort as unique. Therefore, while you might be able to use basic methods and tools again, the situation is different. In reality many IT projects are very similar at a high, strategic level. Where they differ is in the people, exact events — the details. If you read the literature or have been in information systems or IT for some time, you have seen the same reasons for failure and the same problems and issues recur again and again.

Risk is a fuzzy term — it can mean different things to different people. Here, work in IT has a high risk if significant issues remain unresolved or are solved in a way that is negative toward the work. Issues can be either negative problems or positive opportunities. Risk is often characterized as the product of exposure or loss and the likelihood of the problems occurring. By tracking issues, establishing an issues database, and taking other similar steps detailed in this book, you can reduce the likelihood. By being able to address common specific issues in a rapid and consistent manner, you work to reduce both exposure and likelihood.

The foregoing discussion provides the motivating factors behind the writing of this book. Our objectives are to:

• Provide you with a proven, modern method for dealing with IT-related issues and risk.
• Supply an approach for identifying and tracking issues and risk.

- Enable you to perform a wide range of analysis of issues.
- Address specific commonly encountered issues in different areas that include or are related to IT.

How did we identify and select issues that are covered in the book? First, combined we have over 75 years' experience in IT and IT management going back to the 1960s. Second, we have worked with over 150 organizations in over 25 countries and seen all of the issues multiple times. Finally, we have emphasized issues management in seminars and teaching to over 25,000 individuals in over 40 countries.

What are the benefits of all of this? Well, people who have attended our classes and seminars as well as clients have achieved the following benefits.

- Issues are identified earlier — giving more time for solution and action.
- Issues are resolved more consistently because the approach tracks on their repetition.
- You get an early warning of problems in IT work — before the budget or schedule falls apart.
- Management tends to have more realistic expectations, with an awareness of issues.
- Users and managers have greater confidence in IT due to the improved handling of issues.
- Since the number of issues tends to stabilize in an organization, the IT organization and management get better at detecting, preventing, and dealing with issues over time — cumulative improvement.
- Giving attention to issues makes users more realistic in their requests and acts to deter requirement changes and scope creep.

Based on past experience in consulting and teaching, the book should appeal to the following audiences:

- IT managers and staff
- Project leaders
- Business managers and staff involved in IT work
- Consultants and vendors involved in IT

Five parts comprise the book. The first provides the method and tools for dealing with issues. This part answers the following questions.

- Why do IT work and projects run into trouble and fail?
- What constitutes success in issues management?
- What are the benefits of an effective management of issues?
- What are standard measurement techniques of IT work, and why do they fall short?
- What are the types and characteristics of issues?
- Why do the same issues recur again and again?

- How should you identify and describe issues?
- What is an effective issues repository, and how should it be established and maintained?
- How are issues analyzed in single projects and work and across multiple projects?
- What is an effective way to manage issues with vendors and users?
- How should issues be communicated to management — both informally and formally?
- How should issues be managed within IT and overall?
- How do the methods scale up or down depending on the size and scope of the IT organization and its activities?

The next three parts address specific issues in internal operations, external factors, and specific IT activities. Each chapter here deals with an area and provides an introduction with guidelines on how to cope with issues in that area. This is followed by a discussion of each issue. For each issue we discuss:

- How the issue arises and its frequency
- The impact of the issue if not addressed
- How the issue can be detected
- Actions to take if the issue occurs
- How to prevent the issue from becoming a major problem

Examples are also included.

The last part of the book presents the results of a survey of over 200 firms with respect to IT issues. This helped provide the motivation for writing this book. There are also appendices on references, Websites, an index, and a cross-reference (called the magic cross-reference) so that you can easily find something. This last is an alternative to the index.

We have used, and taught others to employ, the methods in the book with great success. Some of the benefits that organizations have achieved are:

- Increased incidence of successful system implementation and business process change
- Reduced cost and schedule for projects and work
- Reduced number of failed projects
- Dropping of bad project ideas due to potential issues
- Early warning of problems before problems occur
- More realistic expectations of what IT can deliver
- Higher morale among IT staff
- Greater collaboration among IT, management, users, and vendors

The methods and guidelines are common sense and jargon free. They have been tested in multiple organizations.

Another note from us: As you read the book, you may find some of the examples unrealistic. You might ask, "Do such companies and organizations exist that are this screwed up?" They do. We and you have knowledge of them or even worked with them. Is this bad? No. It is a fact of life.

We hope you find the guidelines as useful as others with whom we have consulted and who have attended our seminars and classes.

Part I

Issues and Risk Management

Chapter 1

Introduction

COMMON IT-RELATED PROBLEMS

Information systems (IS), or information technology (IT), have been around for over 50 years. The goal of most IS or IT efforts has been to effect change and improvement in business processes and management information. People have been working at this for thousands of years. With all of this experience, you might think that IT work and projects would be very successful if completed on time and within budget.

Too bad. This is still not the case. In the 1980s people were writing that over half (50%) of IT efforts fail. Moreover, among those that are successfully completed, even fewer have resulted in change and improvement. Some recent surveys and one by the authors point to a percentage here of about 30–35% that resulted in tangible, measurable benefits. This is not very good. One disaster story in 2003 was that of a major Japanese bank that had undertaken a major IT project. It was a colossal failure — US$110 million was written off. No salvage. There appears to be little improvement.

Why does this happen? One reason is that technical staff and managers view each IT effort as unique and individual. System development is often viewed as an art or a craft. Lessons learned are gathered, if at all, at the end of a project, when most of the people have vanished to work on other projects and tasks. The experience and lessons learned that were collected were not organized, used, or updated.

The same issues recur again and again. We, the authors, with over 75 years of combined IT experience, have found that the same 100–300 issues or problems are present repeatedly. Here are some examples:

- 110 issues: major logistics firm in Asia
- 145 issues: luxury goods manufacturer
- 209 issues: government agency

If you doubt this, think about the number of times you have heard of the following issues:

- Scope creep
- Changing requirements
- High management expectations of IT
- Lack of user participation

Do these sound familiar? They should. They are just some of the more frequently recurring issues.

Here an issue can be either a problem or opportunity. If work has substantial issues, it has high risk. The issues are the underlying cause for the issues. If you resolve the issues, you mitigate the risk. That is the reason for this book — to provide pragmatic guidelines for managing risk and identifying, preventing, addressing, and measuring these common issues and problems.

If you begin work in IT with a high level of awareness of issues, then life is easier. There are fewer surprises. In IT, we have found surprises are largely negative. The proactive management of issues has proven to provide many benefits for IT organizations we have managed or consulted with.

- Having a common list and approach for many issues means there will be fewer surprise issues.
- There is cumulative improvement, in that a standard issues database is a repository that can be related to any IT effort or project. New issues can be added to the database. If you apply the experience in this database, you can solve issues faster and easier. Moreover, the issues are less likely to recur.
- Having a standardized risk and issues management approach can aid all IT activities — regular work, planning, small projects, support, and large projects.
- Tracking IT work through issues management can provide a much earlier warning system than standard measures of budget versus actual and scheduled versus actual plan.
- Issues awareness can make users, customers, managers, and IT staff more realistic as to what is possible given the purpose and scope of an IT effort.
- Issue detection and resolution improve and are more consistent over time.

WHY IT EFFORTS FAIL

IT efforts fail often for the following reasons.

- Issues are detected too late. Management and staff may not be aware of issues or be looking at the glass as "half full." Here is a lesson learned. Always look at the work as "half empty" — you will achieve more success.
- Issues are not managed well. Typically, issues are managed in an unsystematic, ad hoc manner. Moreover, different managers and leaders may deal with the same issues in different ways. Inconsistency leads to more problems.
- Issues are not tracked using the same measurements of both IT in general and IT project management in particular. This leads to more surprises.
- Experience in resolving issues, doing work, and completing work is not used to improve the management of issues in the future.
- People tend to make the same mistakes again and again with the same issues. This makes measurement, management, and estimation difficult at best and impossible at worse.

There are also problems with the traditional system life cycle. Here are some of them.

- When gathering requirements, it is assumed that users are supportive of the effort and change. This is often not the case. You need to get users to see the need for change.
- Traditionally, you seek to involve a few senior users (called here *king and queen bees*). These people are often the ones who are most resistant to change.
- After the requirements are gathered, users are asked to sign off and approve them. These approvals, as users have learned, are not legally enforceable. We have seen many cases in which users later state that they did not understand or that things have changed. Only with involvement can come commitment to the requirements.
- Users are left alone, sometimes for months. They have seen no results. The requirements gathering could have generated new ideas, resulting in change of scope.
- There is often a disconnect between the training and the implementation of the new system and the current business process. How to get from A to B is not made clear.

Many of the problems stem from a lack of understanding of users and business departments. Let's examine the world from the user point of view. Users each day show up for work and try to get through it. Regardless of IT and projects, the user supervisors still want the employees to get their work done. There is not much incentive to do well in the project or to change.

Then there are the senior users who have been in their departments for years. We will call these individuals *queen and king bees*. They seldom take vacations and have vast knowledge of exceptions. As such, they have tremendous informal power. In some departments the supervisors and managers rely heavily on them to informally manage the work. They are seen by management as a great source of strength. Too bad this is flawed. The king and queen bees often act as barriers to change. In a number of ERP (enterprise resource planning) implementations they supply the business rules to the consultants and IT. If they put in all of the exceptions, the new system may work fine. However, it works just like the old process. What does this add up to? No benefits. However, the king and queen bees as well as the consultants win. Why? King and queen bees get all of their exceptions; consultants get more money, more billable hours.

What is an exception? An exception is a transaction that requires special handling or rules. An exception tends to be a rare event. An example in a standard bank branch is a very large deposit of money or foreign exchange in a strange currency. King and queen bees are often needed to handle this work. Exceptions make king and queen bees important. The more exceptions there are, the more power the king and queen bees have. However, the more exceptions that exist, the less productive and efficient is the department.

To IT, the visible process is seen through the systems provided and supported by IT. However, there is frequently more to the picture than meets the eye. Everyone develops his own shortcuts, tips, and tricks to get things done. It is the same with business departments. When an IT system does not meet their needs, they have to invent solutions. These spreadsheets, databases, or manual systems will be called *shadow systems*. Shadow systems are very important to many users, who may have a substantial investment in them. Shadow systems can also be created to handle new work on an ad hoc basis.

Your body, car, clothes, and apartment or house deteriorate over time. It is the same with business processes. When a new employee is hired, that person is often put into the work and not properly trained in the work. Deterioration sets in. Efficiency drops. Moreover, the new employee can easily fall under the (evil?) influence of the king and queen bees. King and queen bees may create new exceptions to deal with situations. When there are changes in the work, it may be easier to generate a new or modified shadow system than to call on IT and go through another life cycle.

Now you can connect the dots in the foregoing to get an overall picture.

• If the shadow systems are not included in requirements, the users may have to carry them over and even make changes to them to adapt to the new process. What incentive do the users have to do this on their own? Not much.

• If the king and queen bees are able to implement all of the exceptions, then there will be less or no benefit from the new system and process.

Does this sound too cynical? Perhaps, but all too often these things occur. Of course, there are times when the users want change, when the king and queen bees are willing to give exceptions, and when the shadow systems can all be incorporated into the new system. Experience, however, reveals these to be rare events.

IT DIFFERS FROM OTHER TYPES OF BUSINESS WORK

People in IT probably don't think about this much. But it contributes to misunderstandings by management and business employees about IT and IT work. Figure 1.1 shows a table with some of the differences. Let's comment on this table. A business unit employee typically shows up and starts to work. During the day the person completes groups of transactions. Each transaction is a single task. The transactions often are not related. In IT the staff member can be interrupted by questions, crises, and issues. In IT the work is more variable. In network support you encounter a variety of different problems that require problem solving and troubleshooting. In systems work, each system change or requirement has to be analyzed and a solution defined and implemented. The duration of an IT staff member's work is variable; tasks can go on for several days or weeks. For business staff the work tends to be routine, and, since it is finite in duration, it is easy to measure volume, service level, etc. In IT you may not know if a person's work was effective for days or weeks. In the business, an employee can focus on one task or piece of work. From your experience in IT and ours, life is not so simple. There are interruptions.

IT and the business are also different in terms of projects. In standard business projects risk and cost go hand in hand. It is often far different and more deadly in IT. You can see this graphically in Figure 1.2, in which the horizontal axis represents time. There are two curves. The first (solid) shows the expendi-

Factor	Business	IT
Nature of work	Task or transaction	Group of tasks or project
Focus	Short term	Longer term
Concentration	Limited	Problem solving
Activity	Routine work	More variable work
Duration of the work	Transaction, minutes	Longer term, days
Multitasking	Limited	May be extensive
Creativity	Work is routine	Often needed
Measurement	Easy	Difficult

Figure 1.1   Some Key Differences Between IT and Business Work

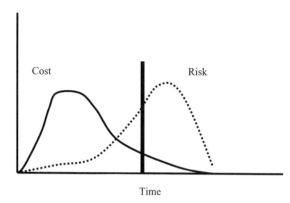

Figure 1.2   Cost and Risk over Time for IT Work

ture of money. In IT you tend to spend much of the funds toward the beginning, with software, hardware, and network components. At the end you have labor hours. Now look at the other curve (dashed), which shows risk. Risk occurs later in the work. Now note the heavy vertical line. This represents about the 90% completion rate. However, the percentage of risk that is completed is less than half, or 50%. The lesson here is that you want project reporting to be sensitive to issues *and* risk.

HOW IT AND THE BUSINESS HAVE CHANGED

Consider the world of business several decades ago. Processes were centered in individual departments. The departments owned their own processes and work. IT was reactive to user requests. IT was like a fire department — responding to successive emergency calls and requests. Life was fairly straightforward.

Things have changed. Processes now cross departments and divisions. There are more interfaces among processes. The boundaries between processes are fuzzier. IT has responded with integrated systems such as ERP systems. Another example that is used in this book is that of Wal-Mart and the rollout of RFID (radio frequency identification) to replace bar coding. Effective RFID implementation requires warehousing, distribution, and the supply chain to be integrated. IT has moved into a coordinating role in implementation. In this new environment, IT responded to management. But what happened to the business departments? In many cases they remained the same. The work changed, but the business organization did not. A single business department does not own a process that crosses three other departments. Who owns the new processes? All of the employees and management. Who increasingly coordinates improvements to the processes? IT.

IT AND POLITICS

As IT has gotten more involved in business processes, IT has become closer to the politics in the organization. In the past many IT groups fell under finance or accounting. Some have said that because of this, many accountants and heads of finance became CEOs — through the use of the information and capabilities of IT.

Today, IT cannot avoid political involvement. How a new system and process are implemented affects the power structure of the winners and losers. Politics sometimes generates new project ideas. Projects can be started and then later killed for political reasons. For example, manager A starts a project. It appears useful, but manager A moves on and is replaced by manager B. Manager B then either changes or kills the project. The new manager is "putting her stamp" on the work.

THE MANAGEMENT VIEW OF IT

Many IT groups have not seen much change in years. IT has often focused on measurement and providing service-level management. Management sees all of this in a different light. In a recent Gartner Group survey, the most interesting finding was that management perceives IT as a bottleneck and even as a barrier to change in the business.

There are many possible reasons for this. First, there may be a perception that IT is overly bureaucratic. Second, some business managers have told us that they view IT as overly formal. A third possible reason is that IT managers have not kept up with the trends in management and processes. A fourth factor is that business managers see IT working on tactical and not strategic projects.

What can we infer about IT from the discussion in the past few sections? One thing is that IT has to become more effective. IT needs to be able to change and deal with resistance to change. IT has to become better at managing and dealing with problems and issues.

ISSUES AND RISK

We have discussed the word *issue* quite a bit. It is not time to discuss it more. An issue is either a problem or an opportunity that can impact the performance of IT and business work and projects. Thus, issues can either be positive or negative. It is the negative issues that we will spend time on, since these often lead to IT failure.

Issues arise at the start of a project or work. New issues appear throughout the work until the end. Even then, issues linger. Issues do not necessarily disappear after they appear to be resolved. People who lost on an issue may not want to give up. They may try to resurrect it. Thus, a lesson learned is that you can never assume that an issue goes away. Be ready for some of the issues to return in a different form.

Now let's turn to risk. Risk can be defined as the possibility of danger, loss, or harm. Mathematically, risk can be viewed as the product of the likelihood of an event and the exposure or loss if the event occurs. Risk is a fuzzy term. Everyone agrees that we need to lessen and control risk. What is behind risk? What is the cause of the risk? It is one or more issues. If the issues are not addressed, the negative event will occur. Hence, you can control the fuzzy risk by dealing successfully with the tangible issues. That is how we will relate issues to risk. If you can deal with the issues, then you reduce the likelihood of the event. If you track and improve your management of issues, you can reduce the exposure.

TYPES OF ISSUES

In the Table of Contents a number of different types of issues have been delineated:

- Internal issues and risk
  - Teams
  - The work
  - Business units
  - Management
  - Projects
  - Resistance to change
- External issues and risk
  - Vendors, consultants, and outsourcing
  - Headquarters
  - International and subsidiaries
  - Technology
  - Business partners
- Issues and risk in specific IT activities
  - Analysis
  - Software packages
  - Development
  - Implementation
  - Operations and support

An issue of one type is different than that of another. Some issues can be controlled within IT or a project team. Other issues are not as controllable. They involve users, vendors, outsiders, or management. There is a big difference

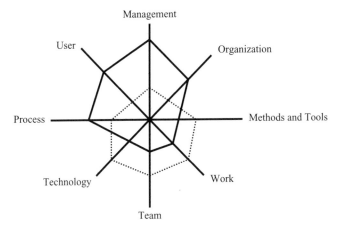

Figure 1.3   Example of Issues, by Type, in a Project

between these two categories. Uncontrolled issues are more complex, generally more political, take longer to resolve, and are sometimes likely to recur again and again.

Another sign of diversity is the range of issues that appear. It is useful to develop a chart of the total number of issues by type. Consider Figure 1.3, which is a spider (or radar) chart. Each dimension is a type of issue. The number of issues is indicated by the distance from the center. The example in the figure includes eight types of issues and two projects. The dashed-line project is the more traditional IT project of the past. The solid-line project is a more modern project, in which the issues are mainly in the business and the process. Notice the difference. The modern project typically has more issues that are out of the control of IT and the team.

THE LIFE CYCLE OF AN ISSUE

Now let us turn to the life cycle of an issue.

• *Symptoms.* You first typically become aware of an issue because of uneasiness, a surprise, or some event. You cannot define the problem, but you know it is there from the symptoms.

• *Issue discovery.* After some time and thought, you discover what you think is the issue. Now you want to get your hands on it.

• *Issue investigation and tracking.* Here you look into different facets of the issue and determine what possible actions and decisions are possible. Since there are multiple issues, you have to do tracking as well.

• *Issue analysis.* With the information in hand, you can now proceed to more in-depth analysis of the issue.

• *Decisions and actions.* A decision and actions will often be required to deal with the issue.
• *Reemergence of the issue.* You thought the issue was solved and that it went away. Think again. The world is political. It can come back — like Freddy in the *Halloween* movies.

SOME COMMON PROBLEMS IN ISSUES MANAGEMENT

Managers often make the same mistakes repeatedly in dealing with issues. Here are some of the common mistakes we have observed.

• People want to jump on the issue and solve it right away. This is a big mistake. If you act too soon, you may find that you acted on the wrong issue. You also may be alerting management to problems too soon. They may see you as "Henny-Penny and the sky falling."
• Decisions are made about issues, but there is a lack of follow-through with actions. The issue remains.
• It is assumed that each issue is unique. This is untrue. Through all of the managing and consulting we have done, a basic truth emerges. The same issues recur again and again. Not all issues apply or appear in any one IT effort, but one issue will likely appear in the same and different organizations and projects many times.
• There is no analysis of issues across multiple projects.
• After decisions and actions, managers assume the issue has been taken care of. However, many issues are political. Losers may try for a rematch.
• You cannot solve issues using one approach. Some people like to see issues in a technical light. This is an excessively narrow focus. In fact, you have to view issues from technical, business, political, managerial, and cultural perspectives.

Issues are like fruit on a tree. They take time to mature and ripen. Through experience you seek to hone your skills of timing in dealing with issues.

ISSUES ACROSS PROJECTS

The same issues can apply to multiple pieces of work or projects. If the separate pieces of work are managed separately, then each occurrence of the issue is addressed separately. This can lead to problems. Solutions can be inconsistent. One solution in one place can affect or undo a solution to the same issue in another area. This applies to both business and IT. Having an organization structured into silos fosters problems in managing issues.

PROBLEMS VERSUS OPPORTUNITIES

Not all issues are bad. Positive opportunities can arise. Here are some examples. A new technology or system may come out. This can lead to substantial business improvement. Another opportunity occurs in a business department if a manager, supervisor, or king or queen bee leaves. This may present a new opportunity for change. A third opportunity is a change in management. You might not have seen eye-to-eye with the old manager, so the management change becomes a new opportunity.

Opportunities also extend into problems. We and you should always try to create new opportunities for improvement by addressing an issue. It would be a shame if you solved the issue and could not get collateral benefits from the effort.

THE GOALS OF IT

With respect to issues and IT management in general, we can define some goals for IT. This book aims to help you achieve these goals.

• You want to have as much high-level standardization as possible. Standardization provides a framework for the work. However, because it is at a high level, you have flexibility in the detail. What can be standardized? Start with issues management and lessons learned. Go then into templates for projects, communications, documentation, and presentations.

• Gather lessons learned as you do the work. Do not wait until the end of the work — do it now, as you go. Lessons learned and issues management are key factors in achieving improvement in IT.

• Implement a systematic approach to issues management. If you implement an issues database and formal issues analysis, reporting, and measurement, you will get on top of the problems. There will be fewer negative surprises.

• Focus on key processes as well as support. IT resources are limited. You cannot support all processes — there are too many. Key to IT success is effective business processes.

• Devote as much IT resources to projects as possible. Each new system or technology requires support. As the support burden grows, you have less time for projects. But projects are the major means to effect business change. Support and maintenance have to be more controlled.

• Be more proactive. IT is often seen as reactive. If IT can get on top of issues earlier, then you move into a proactive state.

• Align to the business. This sounds really good. Every IT manager in the world wants this. How do you do it? By making a difference in the performance of the business processes.

- Solve real issues of users. To users, systems and technology issues often represent a minority of their problems. If IT ignores user issues, then IT can hardly assume that users will embrace change.

PROCESS IMPROVEMENT AND REENGINEERING

In the 1920s a major focus to improve business was industrial engineering. Engineers observed how people worked and suggested improvements. The workers were trained, and the changes were positive. Everything looked bright. A funny thing happened when the engineers revisited the department — the people had reverted to their old habits. There were no benefits and no change.

Was this lesson learned? Hardly, many process improvement and reengineering efforts suffered the same fate. Same with total quality management (TQM), Kaizan, Six Sigma, etc.

Why did this occur? A main reason was that the changes made depended on the people. People change habits slowly. There is deterioration in the work. The people trained in the magic method leave, and the new ones know nothing about the past. Things begin to fall apart.

To obtain structured change, experience reveals that you need IT and systems. Systems and technology provide greater structure for the work. However, if you just implement systems, you may get no change. So IT projects need process improvement. Even with both of these, there can be reversion and deterioration after the improvements. Thus, linked to these is change management. The result is that these three are linked as described in Figure 1.4.

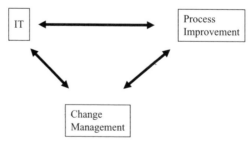

- *IT and process improvement.* You need to improve the work to justify the IT investment. You need IT to get structured change.
- *IT and change management.* To be successful, it is necessary to address resistance to change. Change management to be lasting needs IT.
- *Process improvement and change management.* Changing a process is not enough to prevent reversion — you need more formal change management.

Figure 1.4 Linkage Between IT, Process Improvement, and Change Management

GENERAL APPROACH TO ISSUES AND RISK MANAGEMENT

The approach is this book begins with Figure 1.4. That is why many of the issues discussed later deal with change and resistance to change. For these three to be successful, you have to implement a structured issues management approach. The critical success factors here consist of the following elements.

• *Issues databases that are employed across all IT efforts and projects.* The databases provide a repository for the problems and opportunities.

• *Collaboration.* In dealing with issues, you must involve others in order to gain political support for the later decisions and actions.

• *Early identification of issues.* Getting potential issues out on the table makes people more realistic about work and projects.

• *Active issues tracking and analysis.* A more structured approach is necessary for examining and assessing issues.

• *Issues reporting and communications.* Just like work status, you have to communicate about issues with management, users, vendors, and IT staff.

• *Cumulative improvement.* As you solve the same issues again and again, you find that you get better at issues management. You also gain experience and learn lessons that help your overall effectiveness.

When we have gone into an organization to turn around an IT group, we implemented these things. The benefits of this are evident. First, IT work becomes more predictable — less of an art, more as production. Second, management sees that you are on top of the issues, and so you gain their respect. Third, through collaboration you achieve a better working relationship with managers, users, IT staff, and others. Fourth, you reduce the risk and chance of failure — thereby improving the likelihood of your success.

ORGANIZATION OF THE BOOK

The book has four parts and several appendices.

• Part I lays out an effective approach to issues and risk management. Chapter 2 establishes the structure for issues management. Chapter 3 presents methods for analyzing issues.

• Part II deals with internal issues and risk. We begin with team and work issues and then move onto business users, management, and projects. Of interest in light of the discussion in this chapter is the last chapter in Part II (Chapter 9), which deals with resistance to change.

• Part III addresses external issues and risk. With the widespread use of outsourcing, it is not a revelation that the first chapter here (Chapter 10) deals with vendors, consultants, and outsourcing. Chapter 11 addresses issues relating to headquarters. More firms are international. Headquarters directives and their role can generate major issues. Chapter 12 focuses on technology. With supply chain integration, suppliers and customers are more closely intertwined.

• Part IV centers attention on areas of IT. Included here are strategic planning, analysis, software packages, development, implementation, and operations and support.

Parts II through IV have the same format. The assessment of each issue begins with a discussion of the issue in general. Examples are given, along with how the issue arises and its frequency. The second area is that of impacts of the issue to IT, business units, the processes, and management. This is followed by a discussion on how to prevent the issue from occurring. The final part covers actions to take if the issue surfaces as well as how to prevent the issue from occurring.

There are four appendices.

• *The Results of a Survey on IT Issues.* This appendix helped motivate the book. It contains the results of an international survey of over 200 firms in 20 countries and 40 industries and government agencies.

• *The Magic Cross-Reference.* This has proven to be more useful than the index in helping you locate topics quickly.

• *Websites.* These are useful Websites on change management, issues, IT management, and process improvement.

• References

Finally, there is an index.

CONCLUSIONS

Managing issues is an integral part of IT management. To be successful in IT, you have to be able to successfully cope and address a wide variety of issues. To achieve business improvement, you have to overcome many user, managerial, political, and cultural issues.

If undertaken successfully, issues and risk management lead to cumulative improvement in IT. A key benefit here is that experience shows that there are fewer surprises if you manage the issues well. As you probably are aware, many surprises are not pleasant. By managing issues, you manage the resulting risks.

Our experience also shows that if you can better manage issues, you will have more enjoyment, less stress, and more fun in doing work related to IT.

Chapter 2

Effective Issues Management and Coordination

INTRODUCTION

The stage for issues management was set in the preceding chapter. Here we turn to the details of how to coordinate and address issues. At the core of this is the establishment of a central set of issues databases that are employed throughout IT. Here are some of the factors you will be overcoming within IT:

• *Resistance by some IT staff* who still think each project and effort is unique. Therefore, the issues are unique.
• *Compartmentalization within IT.* Different IT groups may have little contact with each other, even when they are only feet or cubicles apart.
• *Lack of awareness of issues.* Many do not label and track the issues.

This occurred recently in a software development organization we worked with in Asia. There were three IT development groups, each assigned to develop and support users in different countries. There was little contact between the groups, even though they were all located in the same area.

In the first meetings the lack of communications and awareness of issues became evident. A workshop was conducted in which each group made a list of issues they had encountered. Some examples were given to start them out. They were given about 30 minutes to develop a list. They did not have to solve the issues; nor did they have to analyze them. They just had to list them.

Once the issues were written down, a major overlap between the groups was obvious. In the end there were 78 issues. All of the employees agreed that these were the most commonly encountered problems. There were customer, subcontractor, management, technical, and project issues. These became the start of the issues database. Since then the number of issues has grown to 97, but no new issues have been uncovered in the last three months.

The organization has implemented the issues management approach developed in this chapter and the analysis methods of the following chapter. So far they have realized the following benefits.

• Potential issues are discussed with customers and users at the start of the work. This has helped increase the user role. Moreover, the expectations for the work are more realistic and the scope is more precise.

• Issues are tracked across the groups. The same approach is used for the issue in each group. Management and staff time are saved because the same issue has to be solved fewer times.

• The project leaders now provide issues reporting to management on a weekly basis. This has prevented a major crisis in one project already. There is common agreement that, had they waited until the budget and schedule deteriorated, the project could not have been saved.

• The issues database has led to lessons learned and project templates. There are now standardized project templates for 35 major IT activities and over 250 lessons learned.

• With the establishment of the issues databases, collaboration between the groups is now greater at all levels. Success here triggered lessons learned meetings.

GENERAL MANAGEMENT OF ISSUES

Beyond the issues databases themselves, you have to embed issues awareness and tracking throughout almost all IT management and project activities. These include:

• Identification of potential issues at the start of an effort
• Definition of issues as they arise and association of these with the issues databases
• Coordination of issues for which vendors, users, and others are responsible
• Tracking of issues in terms of actions and results
• Analysis of issues within and across IT projects and work (covered in the next chapter)
• Reporting on the issues to management, users, etc.
• Informal communications with management, users, vendors, etc. on issues

You want to have an organized approach for each of these bullets. Otherwise, the tendency is to revert back to addressing issues in an ad hoc manner.

- Open
- Closed
- Potential
- Combined with another issue
- Tabled (the issue is there, but nothing is required)

These data elements support the analysis of issues covered in the next chapter.

The issues databases link to databases for lessons learned. This is because you can use experience in the lessons learned database to help resolve issues. There are three lessons learned databases. The first is the core lessons learned database. The second is a cross-reference to projects and tasks. The third provides for the updating of the lessons learned through application. The data elements for these are given in Figures 2.1–2.3. The third database allows and supports the improvement of the lessons learned over time.

Some amplifying comments on the lessons learned databases are useful. As with issues, you need to be able to link them to the work. This is one of the reasons why project and work templates are useful.

These databases do not maintain themselves. There is a need for a coordination role to do this. In the example given in the introduction and in over 60 other organizations, a useful method is to assign the coordination to two people (typically senior analysts or some project leaders). These individuals do their normal work as well, so this is in addition. The two individuals serve for 4–6 months in this role. There is overlap — the term of one person overlaps that of the other by several months so as to transfer knowledge.

One advantage of this approach is that the coordination eventually falls on many people. All of the analysts and project leaders eventually gain experience in coordinating issues and lessons learned. This helps them to be more effective in their work. A second advantage is that, with assignments, there is also no establishment of a bureaucracy. The last thing you need is more of that. A third benefit is that different people see issues and lessons learned differently, so you get a variety of viewpoints over time.

GETTING STARTED

OK, it sounds good. But how do you start? What is the easiest way to create the database with the least effort and pain? You could gather people together and with a blank tablet in hand ask for their issues. You will likely be met with blank stares and grumbling. Not good.

A better approach is to take the Table of Contents, which lists many issues, as a start. Circulate the list prior to the meeting. Ask people to comment on the list. Here are some questions to pose.

- Which issues in a group give the most problems?
- How frequently do some of the issues arise?
- How many people in the meeting have experienced the same issue?
- What actions have they found useful in dealing with the issue?

This initial discussion will likely trigger more issues from the group. Figure 2.4 gives the initial list for the example company discussed in the introduction.

- Customer/user issues
  — No appropriate subject method expert
  — Lack of available resources
  — Openness of team to suggestions
  — Users not knowing data quality
  — Unqualified customer staff
  — Users not using the fields they have correctly
  — Insufficient resources available
  — Lack of understanding of business rules
  — Users not signing off
  — Big surprise when you demonstrate the work
  — Lack of information on current system — need for validation
  — Specification not signed off
  — Lack of understanding of business
  — Language translation problems
  — Requirement changes — when you show users what they will get, involve as many users as possible
  — Staff turnover among customers
  — Users resisting change
  — Senior users not supporting the project
  — Users indicating that they are too busy to participate in the project
  — Users lacking standardized procedures
  — Users not cooperating with each other
  — System owner wanting system in conflict with users
  — Users putting pressure on for immediate attention
- Management issues
  — Dependencies on systems if there's no agreement on schedule
  — Inadequate time to generate test data
  — Availability of resources
  — People not tracking their issue performance
  — Outstanding problems not treated with high priority
  — Time difference between countries
  — Language issues
  — Staff turnover in IT
  — High management expectations
  — Skill mismatch
  — Lack of funding
  — Delays in related projects impact tasks
  — Too much of the project depends on external organizations that cannot be controlled
  — No follow-up after decisions
  — Significant top management change

- Project and planning issues
  - Tasks more sequential than was planned
  - Too much detail in the plan
  - Purpose of the project unclear at the start
  - Expanding scope of the project
  - With expanding scope, no budget or resource addition
  - People unwilling to change the structure of the project
  - Plan not synchronized with actual results
  - Need for organized approach to deal with contingencies
  - Too much rework in the project
  - No one seeing how the work is being done to look for improvements
  - Too many unplanned tasks
- Technical and systems issues
  - Data not current
  - Excessive manual data entry required
  - Old system lacking documentation; no knowledge; no valid source code
  - Limited understanding of the application
  - Lack of understanding of best practices
  - Conversion using new technology
  - Insufficient range of test data
  - Modules not functioning properly
  - Test environment not realistically representing the production setting — risk assessment
  - Poor sample data
  - Misunderstanding of functionalities
  - Quality of the work
- Subcontractor issues
  - Vendor delivering poor-quality software
  - Vendor saying you did not give enough time
  - Vendor with competing priorities
  - Wrong vendor selected
  - Miscommunication between vendor project leader and their own staff
  - Finding a vendor who can do the job for the price
  - Project slippage due to vendor lack of delivery
  - Vendor closing up/going out of business before the end of the work
  - Vendor contract unworkable
  - Vendor changing staff frequently
  - Vendor not sharing information with employees
  - Vendor unwilling to work on joint tasks with employees
  - Vendor using different methods or tools than we do
  - Vendor not responding quickly to issues

Figure 2.4   Examples of Issues from the Example Firm

DEFINING ISSUES AT THE START OF PROJECTS AND WORK

When new work is conceived, you want to identify potential issues. Otherwise, the appearance of each issue can be an unpleasant surprise. You can begin to do this by producing a checklist of issues from the database. You politically want the managers, users, etc. to recognize and begin to own the issues. Here is a good approach. Identify more issues than you think will occur. Circulate the list, with the caveat that these have not occurred, but given the purpose and scope of the work it is possible they will occur. This shows them that you are just being realistic and not negative.

Take one issue and discuss how it could be addressed. This will begin to establish an issues analysis and resolution method. Included here is issue escalation. It is much better to do this now than later. Later, you will have a real issue that could be politically charged and people will be in no mood to abstractly discuss how to resolve issues. Separate the issues resolution and escalation definition for the solution of any issue.

As you can experience, you can associate groups of issues with the type of work. Some issues, of course, can apply to all types of work. Having this association can make life easier. We have used this approach in doing development, software package implementation, and other work. It shows to people that you are experienced and are actively using the experience to plan the work.

After you have defined the issues, you can enter these in the project issues database. You can match up each of the issues to the tasks in the project plan. This will validate that the tasks in the plan are complete. If you find an issue with no corresponding task, you can add the task.

You can trade off the scope with the issues. Refer to Figure 1.3, in which we used a spider, or radar, chart to consider the issues by type. If you narrow the scope, then the potential issues will likely diminish. If you widen the scope, then the number or severity of issues grows. This can be valuable to management in setting the proper scope at the start of the work. Obviously, if the scope is too narrow, there are few issues but also almost no benefits.

Next, go to the list of tasks in the project plan and ask if there are any issues in the work. If there are and the issue is not in the list of issues, you can add the issue. In this way you can validate that the list of issues is complete.

There is a political reason for doing this. We have seen disaster happen in the same way many times. The project leader tells management that an issue is critical. The manager says, "OK, now show me which tasks have this issue so that I can see the impact of the issue on the plan." If the project leader has not done this, he or she looks somewhat like a fool!

We have even used the initial issues to kill a potential project. Here is what happened. Management was given a list of potential issues. The likelihood that the issues would occur was discussed and was deemed high. The nature of the issues was very political. It was clear that the managers lacked sufficient power or authority to address the issues. The project idea was quietly killed. This is much better than blundering along and starting the project — only later to have the project blow up in their faces.

TRACKING OF ISSUES AND RISK

After an issue has been identified, it should be analyzed. Answer the following questions.

- Can the issue wait for more information?
- What is the nature of the issue — technical, managerial, political, etc.?
- What is the importance of the tasks that relate to the issue?
- What are related issues?

An issue is assigned to someone for investigation. This is often done on a casual basis. It is not surprising that the person to whom the issue is assigned looks at the issue from his or her own point of view. For example, a person grounded in technology will often view the issue in a technical context. As you have seen in work, many issues have managerial, cultural, and political facets. A technical solution might fail. When an issue is assigned, there should be a discussion of the issue from different perspectives. Here are some things to cover.

- The urgency of the issue — what happens if nothing is done?
- The importance of the issue — the impact of solving the issue
- The issue from different views
  — Technical
  — Managerial
  — Political
  — Cultural
  — Organizational
  — Process

You also might want to have the person think of some possible options that spur creative thinking. These include:

- Do nothing about the issue — gather more information.
- Throw money or resources at the issue.
- Try to solve the issue with systems and technology.
- Try to solve the issue through procedures, policies, or some nonmonetary means.
- Make the issue go away by merging it with something else.

Look at the impact of an unresolved issue from different perspectives.

- Direct effect on the related tasks
- Impact on the team
- Effect on the users
- Visibility to management
- Impact on other issues

When the person returns from looking into the issue, it is a good idea to probe not only what the person did, but also how she or he approached the issue. One method is first to discuss if the issue is getting worse in terms of impact. If nothing is changing, maybe a decision can wait. If the situation is deteriorating, then you can uncover the factors behind the decline. Also, review the sources

of information the investigator used. Next, turn to the range of alternative decisions they considered.

Here are some additional guidelines for investigating an issue.

- See if the issue is part of a bigger problem.
- Determine if other projects or work have the same issue.
- Find any issues that have a lot in common with this issue.
- Determine if this is an issue that has resurfaced.
- Separate out the symptoms from the problem.

When an issue arises, you begin to track it. As we said in the last chapter,
this does not mean plunge in and solve it. You might begin to investigate
the issue. However, there are often too many issues to deal with at one time.
Here are some of the criteria you could employ to select the issues to pursue.
Note that these things are subjective — based on your knowledge and
experience.

- *Importance of the issue.* What is the impact of the issue if it is not
solved?
- *Clarity of definition of the issue.* Is the issue clearly defined, and do
people agree on this definition?
- *Urgency of the issue.* Are there immediate negative effects if you do not
address the issue?
- *Visibility of the issue.* This is an important political element.

How should you proceed? Use the same approach you would at home with
household issues. If a problem is not clear, you will likely not want to solve it.
You will wait for more information. This occurs with your car if it makes a
strange sound but otherwise appears OK.

The issue can be very important. However, if you do not solve it today, it
will still be there tomorrow. Issues that require major life decisions fall into
this category. Rushing into a marriage is one example.

The most widely used criterion is urgency. If you do not do something now,
there will be an immediate impact and it will not be good. That is how doctors
get you to agree to operations. A surgical procedure is dangerous. You could
die of infection or acquire a disease in the hospital. The surgery will put you
out of work and will cost money — even with insurance. Finally, you will be
in a great deal of pain and discomfort. How has any doctor for thousands of
years gotten people to agree to suffer all of this? Fear and urgency. If you do
not have the procedure, you could really be sick. You could even die. If it works
for them, it works for us.

Tracking issues means that each week and day we have to be aware of the
major outstanding, unresolved issues and problems. This state of mind is necessary so that you will not give up or let down your guard on issues. You will
tend to see the glass as half empty. Thus, even when there is great success and

achievement in the work, you will always be thinking of issues. If things appear too good to be true, they often are.

USER AND VENDOR ISSUE COORDINATION

During most IT efforts, users and/or vendors are assigned issues to address. If this is done without planning, it may be difficult to track the open issues. Moreover, tracking issue performance will be more complex. A proven approach is to create a central list of issues for everyone involved in the work. This means that the only legitimate issues are those on this list. This provides control.

In tracking the issues, you should hold regular meetings with each vendor or user group to go over issues. Try to make this a separate meeting from status, because status might muddy the discussion of issues.

ISSUE AND RISK COMMUNICATIONS AND REPORTING

You need to have standard methods for communicating with people about issues and risk. Without an organized approach, you will probably omit some critical information. When people realize that you have a standard approach, they will easily understand the structure of the communications and will more quickly turn to the content of what is said.

Let us first consider formal communications. In IT there are only a small number of possible presentations.

- *New project or work idea.* Here you would discuss the potential problems that might be encountered in the work. You could also give several alternative versions of purpose and scope and see how the issues change.
- *Status of the work.* You want to discuss what major open issues exist. You can also discuss urgency and importance. How much of the work with issues that remains and that has been completed should also be presented.
- *IT overall or multiple projects.* You can start with a summary GANTT chart in which you provide a summary of scheduled versus actual. Then you could show the summary tasks along with tasks that have issues. This tends to make management or any audience more aware of the issues. Following this you can present a table of issues versus projects. The table entry is the impact of the issue on the specific project.

If you are comparing the state of two projects, you could use the spider, or radar, chart in Figure 2.5. Here the dimensions of the chart are the types of

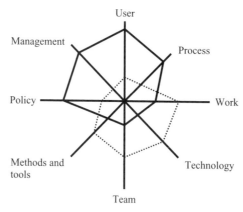

Figure 2.5 Comparison of Two Projects in Terms of Open Issues (Project A — solid lines; Project B — dashed lines)

issues. The distance from the center represents the number of open issues at the time. In this figure, project A appears to have the greatest risk, since most of the open issues are not within the scope and control of the project.

• *Specific issue or group of issues.* Here you can start with a GANTT chart showing summary tasks and all tasks that link to the tasks that have the issue. This demonstrates the time importance. Next, you can examine potential alternative solutions, as was discussed earlier.

• *Results from a project or work.* Obviously, you would give the purpose, scope, schedule, and benefits achieved. It is also useful to summarize the issues that were addressed. After all, there may have been additional benefits from resolving the issues.

Now let's turn to informal communications. What is the best way to communicate on issues? In person. Next, telephone. Why? Because there is no written record. No trail. Also, you can convey tone of voice, body language, etc. E-mail or faxes rank very, very low. If you attempt to discuss an issue through e-mail, you should politically sanitize what you write. You should assume that everyone involved will read what you write. When you do this, your writing will often seem stale and dry. E-mails tend to live a long time, so be very careful. When you are supervising a team or group, make ground rules about communicating on issues very clear. We have seen groups get into real trouble because someone wrote a flaming e-mail about an issue.

Consider meetings with managers. If every time you meet with a manager you have issues, then the manager will almost dread seeing you. "Here comes the IT manager with another list of problems." Try to see managers one-on-one every few weeks. You can give status and a story. If you mention an issue, indicate that they do not need to do anything; you are just keeping them informed. They like the information. You are not putting them on the spot to resolve problems. They can think about the issue calmly later. In later meetings, you can update them on the issues and gradually build up to decisions and actions. This is much calmer that just blurting out an issue.

When you have issues, go with more than one issue. If a manager is faced with one issue, he or she errs on the side of caution and will not want to make a decision. You could go with three issues. The first issue is a simple one that the manager can easily solve. The manager feels good and there is a pattern of success. The second issue is a politically impossible and intractable issue that neither you nor the manager can solve. The manager feels guilty or at least bad that this could not be addressed. Now present the third issue. Often, the manager will make a real effort to solve this issue.

HANDLING ISSUES WITHIN THE IT ORGANIZATION

Many issues occur within an IT group. Some managers like to keep the issues to themselves and not discuss them with the employees. They might think that the staff members are not mature enough to talk about political issues. They may feel that discussing an issue might disturb the work. An IT manager in the Middle East followed this approach. The general manager and the head of finance led the drive to implement a new finance system. It was successfully installed, but it was resisted by five king bees. They kept using the old system. The general manager told the king bees that the old system could no longer be supported. The king bees were not dumb. They decided to take the programmer for the old system out to a huge feast. The IT manager had not informed the programmer of the issue. When asked by the king bees if he could continue to support the old system, he responded, "Of course. No problem." Management was undermined. This led to a two-month political project to undermine the king bees.

What should you do? Take meetings that deal with status and summarize the status. Spend the rest of the time discussing issues or gathering lessons learned. When you discuss an issue, you are raising the political and cultural awareness of the employees. This is good. In the meeting, you will not attempt to resolve the issue. Issues resolved under pressure in meetings often lead to bad decisions and actions. Using this approach, the IT staff will not be as politically naïve. Do not attempt to solve the issue in the meeting. This will just create more pressure and likely lead to bad solutions. These might have to be undone later.

DECISION MAKING AND FOLLOW-UP

Having a range of alternative decisions to consider has been covered. Instead of making the decision, jump to actions that stem from the decisions. Sometimes, decisions are fuzzy. Actions are always precise. If you consider the potential actions on the issue, you gain insight into the possible decisions and the issue itself. If the actions do not appear to be feasible, then that reflects on the decision.

If you feel that the issue will return or reemerge, then you might not want to make a decisive move. You may want to implement only part of the actions that are consistent with the decision. Why? Because if you pursue all of the actions, you could find that when the issue comes back, you have very few options.

Remember too that many people have their own agendas that they do not reveal. When considering decisions and actions, assume that these exist. Put yourself in their shoes and ask how you would respond.

Now suppose that a decision has been made. Should you rush out and announce it? Don't do that. Here are some guidelines to consider.

• Announce the decision and the actions. If the atmosphere is very political and you are only going to carry out some of the actions, then protect your options and reveal only that part of the decision that pertains to the actions. This may sound devious, and some might think it is. But we live in a political world.

• When you make known the decisions and actions, always indicate what the expected or anticipated results are supposed to be. This will help the individuals who have to implement the actions. It serves better to set expectations.

• Make sure that you take the actions immediately after they are announced. The United States has had presidents who announced decisions but did not take actions. This created more confusion than if the decision had not been announced. The president appeared weak after that.

• Follow up on the actions. Try to have most actions taken in 48 hours or less. If the actions stretch out in time, then there may be credibility problems. How people interpret the actions may be questioned.

DEALING WITH MULTIPLE ISSUES

Very seldom will you have one issue in isolation. The issue may be part of an overall pattern. It is the same with children. If you see one instance of bad behavior, there are probably going to be others. And there is an underlying pattern and reason for the behavior. It is the same with issues.

Chapter 3

Analysis and Measurements of Issues and Risk

INTRODUCTION

This chapter focuses on measurements and analysis of issues and risk in IT, projects, and work. In the last chapter, you saw that tracking and managing issues not only are good for preventing failure, but also aid in preventing major problems before they worsen. Keep in mind that the basis for the analysis are the issues databases.

We have some specific political goals in this chapter.

- Alert managers and others to problems in advance so that there are no surprises.
- Identify issues early so as to have more time for solutions or to be able to take action faster.
- Increase issues awareness to make people more realistic about the work.
- Deal with issues more openly.

This chapter contains a number of measurements and charts relating to issues and risk. How should you use these? You should use them just as we do when we enter an organization to evaluate their projects. You can employ the issues analysis methods here to predict which projects will be or are in the greatest peril. With these tools and methods, you have in effect an early warning system of risk.

PROBLEMS WITH STANDARD MEASUREMENTS

Let's start with a project. It has a budget and a schedule. So you could track budget versus actual and schedule versus actual. That is what everyone does. However, as you saw in the first chapter, the costs of the project that do not include labor are normally included at the start of the work. You need the hardware, network, and software so that you can do development, testing, and integration. The rest of the costs are labor hours. Labor in many projects peaks during development. If you look at the cost distribution of a construction project, the acquisition cost for the land is up front. Material and labor costs continue throughout most of the rest of the schedule. Even after the basic structure is assembled, there is the build-out and finish work. Consider building a house. A high percentage of the cost is in building the kitchens and bathrooms.

Turn your attention now to schedule versus planned. The schedule looks fine. Then, suddenly, the project schedule slips. What happened? Here are some common events.

- There was a problem.
- People tried to deal with and it failed.
- The schedule is adjusted.

Time is lost. There is less time to deal with the issue. The problem is more visible due to delay in the schedule. There is more pressure. You could appear to be a bad manager, since you were surprised.

In standard projects, concepts such as activity-based costing and earned value and cost make a great deal of sense. They really can reveal what is going on overall and can help pin down problems. If things go wrong, then there are often added material and labor costs. It is different in IT. Since most of the costs have been incurred early, the remainder of the project consumes labor hours.

Now let's make a switch in terminology. We and you should never call a project involving IT an IT project unless it deals totally with infrastructure. The reason is political. If you call a project an IT project, then the users may opt out and will not feel accountable for benefits. However, here it is simpler to call it an IT project.

In an IT project if something goes wrong, it tends to happen later in the work. When you are gathering requirements, doing design, or acquiring software packages, there is not much risk. In truth you do not know enough yet. You don't know in the IT project whether:

- The requirements are really right. You can get unpleasant surprises when you deliver the system or even a prototype.
- The software package does not cover enough of the business work, so you have to invent shadow systems or attempt to modify the package.

Issues	Project 1	Project 2	Project 3
14			
15			

Figure 3.4   Sample Issues-Versus-Projects Table

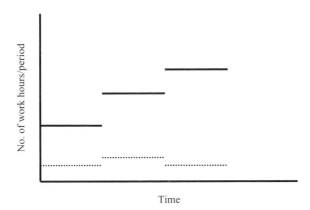

Figure 3.5   Example of Risk Distribution over Time for Project A

- *Percentage of remaining work with issues and risk.* You can get at this in Microsoft Project by filtering on risky tasks in the future or active tasks. Then you can select the Resource Usage view. This can be exported to a spreadsheet. Do the same for the overall project and you can get the percentage. This is a key measure for comparing project performance and also a good way for managers to direct their problem-solving time.
- *Earned risk.* You are familiar with earned work and earned cost. Earned risk is similar. You can use filtering and the Resource Usage view to get the number of hours of work associated with completed tasks with issues to calculate earned risk. Earned risk is useful in comparing multiple projects.
- *Distribution of risk and issues over time.* Each period of time, such as a month or a week, has a total number of hours of work. In this period some lesser number of hours is associated with risk. So you can plot the distribution of risk over time.

Let's consider two examples. In Figure 3.5 you can see the distribution of one project (A) over time. Figure 3.6 contains the distribution of a second project (B). In each figure the solid line indicates the total number of hours of work in the period. The dotted line indicates the number of hours of work associated with risky tasks or tasks with issues. As you can see, Project A has more hours and so is the larger project. Normally, management would give more attention to this project because of size. However, this is fundamentally wrong. You should give more attention to Project B since more of its work is risky.

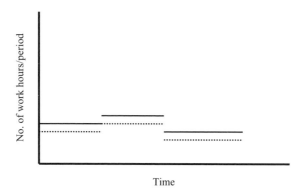

Figure 3.6   Example of Risk Distribution over Time for Project B

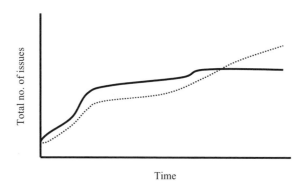

Figure 3.7   Total Number of Issues

TOTAL ISSUES

This section and the next four generate graphs that can easily be obtained from the project issues database of Chapter 2. It is useful to plot the total number of issues that surface in a project. Figure 3.7 contains two graphs. The solid curve represents a fairly typical case in which the number of issues rises and then levels off. Toward the end there are not too many new issues. The dotted curve reveals a project in trouble. The number of issues keeps growing. Not good. The project will either fail or be in very serious difficulty.

OPEN ISSUES

Open issues can be more revealing than the total number of issues. Figure 3.8 plots the number of open issues over time. The solid line represents a good project. The number of open issues initially rises as more issues are discovered. Then it drops as issues are solved. It continues to drop until implementation,

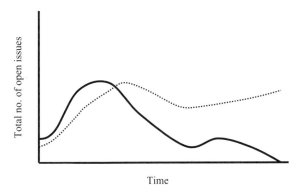

Figure 3.8   Total Number of Open Issues over Time

when it rises again with some of the issues we discussed earlier. Then it falls off. Issues discovered at the end got a lot of effort and attention to resolve quickly. The dotted line characterizes a project in trouble. While the number of open issues rises and then falls, the number of open issues does not fall rapidly. Then the number of open issues increases. Watch out — failure is ahead.

Figure 3.8 is useful to compare multiple projects or even to analyze one project. You can see by the rate of decline how the project is coping with issues. Moreover, when the number of open issues starts to increase, you know there are problems. This is an early warning system.

UNCONTROLLED VERSUS CONTROLLED OPEN ISSUES

In the previous two chapters, we identified various types of risk. Some of these were controllable within the project and IT; others were external to the work. Using the project issues database, you can construct the charts in Figure 3.9. Here you see a project in trouble. The controlled issues behave well. Even though there are more open ones overall, they are still solved in the end. The dotted line for the uncontrolled issues tells a different story. There the number of open, uncontrolled issues grows toward the end.

AGING OF OPEN ISSUES

You can create the charts in Figure 3.10 from the project issues database. Each issue has a discovery date. You can plot the percentage of open issues by discovery date over time. In this case, the percentage of issues that are open and that were just discovered is 100%. In a successful project this percentage

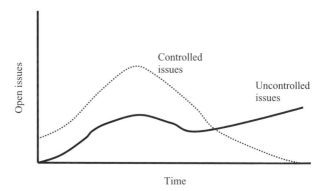

Figure 3.9   Uncontrolled versus Controlled Open Issues

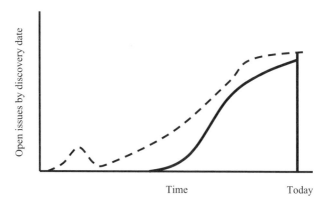

Figure 3.10   Aging of Open Issues over Time

declines as you go back in time. This is indicated by the solid line. The dotted line is quite different. Here you can see a bubble in the past. This represents several significant issues that remain unresolved. Use this chart to compare projects, and you should get a great deal of management interest.

AVERAGE TIME TO RESOLVE ISSUES

Another way to compare project performance is based on the average time to solve an issue. Figure 3.11 gives two charts. The solid line indicates a well-behaved project. The average time rises as the project leader and others deal with issues. Then it drops as they get better at dealing with issues. It increases slightly as implementation approaches. Issues found toward the end are resolved fast. The dotted line typifies a project in trouble. The average time for issue

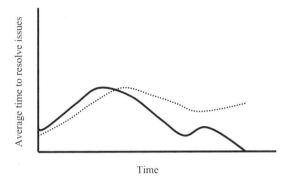

Figure 3.11   Average Time to Resolve Issues

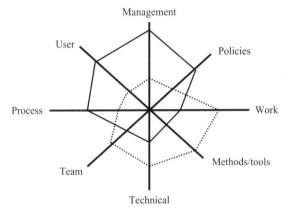

Figure 3.12   Distribution of Open Issues by Type

resolution drops but then rises. This reveals that it is taking longer to resolve the later-discovered issues.

You can use this approach to compare the time to resolve issues by type. Alternatively, you can compare uncontrolled and controlled issues. Politically, you can use these charts to show project leaders how they are doing in managing issues.

DISTRIBUTION OF OPEN ISSUES BY TYPE

It is useful to assess IT work based on the number of open issues by type. Figure 3.12 gives the distribution for two projects. Note that such a snapshot can be created at any time. Thus, it may not be the case that these are two projects. The charts could be the same project at different points in time. The

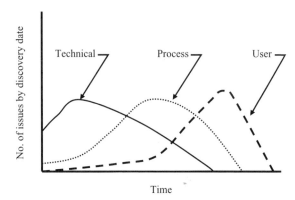

Figure 3.13   Issues by Type by Discovery Date over Time

difference between the two projects is more than academic. For the solid-line project, the open issues are mainly uncontrolled. The opposite is true of the dotted-line project. You can use this chart to zero in on which projects need more attention than others.

There is another use of this chart. Suppose you are comparing several potential projects. One method of comparison is to assess the likely issues and problems each will face. Since you identified these potential issues when the projects were conceived, you can develop Figure 3.12 for these potential projects. This is a good aid in project selection.

ISSUES BY TYPE OVER TIME

Let's consider three types of issues: technical, process, and user. You can plot the number of issues by each type by discovery date over time. The result is shown in Figure 3.13. Here the technical issues often appear first. This is shown by the solid line. Many are known at the start. Next, process issues, such as exceptions and shadow systems, make their appearance (shown by the dotted line). Toward the end you have resistance to change and other related issues (the dashed line). This chart provides management with a better understanding of issues and shows that uncontrolled issues often appear later, another reason why projects fail.

SELECTION OF ISSUES FOR DECISIONS AND ACTIONS

At any given time you must decide among the open issues which ones to make decisions and take actions on. Figure 3.14 can help you do this. Here the

better and more credible grounds for termination. Here are some guidelines for termination.

- The mix of unresolved issues is strongly biased toward uncontrolled issues.
  - The trend in open issues is not good.
  - The average time to resolve issues has not dropped.
  - More issues are being discovered each day or week.
  - Old, open, unresolved major issues remain.

CONCLUSIONS

Many articles and books talk about risk and issues. They often dissociate issues from risk. We have shown that they are deeply intertwined. Next, much of the discussion in the literature is fuzzy and subjective. The framework for effective issues and risk management was laid out in the previous chapter. This chapter presented to you a variety of methods for analyzing and assessing risk and issues in a more structured way that will garner more user, management, and IT support.

Part II

Internal Issues and Risk

Internal issues are those that are largely contained within IT, its work and projects. As such, they have characteristics that make them easier to solve while at the same time being more frequent. Experience shows that if the IT management and organization are more aware of these issues, they can be more easily prevented, detected, and acted on.

The issues have been organized into the following areas.

- *Teams.* Anyone who has either worked or managed in IT realizes that IT staff are quite different from those in standard business units. We have found in managing a variety of different IT groups in various industries and countries that the same issues recur again and again.
- *Work.* IT work is different than standard business work. There is support, maintenance, enhancements, projects — a wider variation than found in typical business departments. Variety, while more interesting, creates more challenges.
- *Business units.* The role of business units in IT work can often spell the difference between success and failure. Working to build and sustain an effective business unit is a challenge made easier by being able to effectively deal with frequent and common issues.
- *Management.* Management issues often dominate the internal issues. They are more complex and political to address.
- *Projects.* Critical to IT success is the effective completion of projects. In many organizations the only way that improvements occur is through projects.
- *Resistance to change.* This is a separate category, since experience shows it is a major area for IT failure. Many systems are completed and installed successfully. However, there is no business change, so the benefits are found to be either short-lived or nonexistent.

Chapter 4

Teams

INTRODUCTION

Having managed hundreds of IT and business staff over the years, we can say that we have seen many different personnel and team-related issues. There have been only two really genius programmers. Everyone seems to seek these people out. There is the misconception that somehow if they could be found and put on your team, life would be good and the work would be completed earlier and with less effort. Not true! One guy dressed in black, drove a black motorcycle, and lived in a house in which all of the furniture, walls, floors, etc. were black. Is that weird, or what? He was exceptional. He created a system for an insurance company in record time. Later, he had a motorcycle accident and decided to become a doctor. The insurance company called and wanted some changes. Since he was not available, we suggested they contact a major systems firm. They did and it took over three months for them to figure out how he did the programming and design.

The other genius fellow spent his spare time reading Microsoft, IBM, and Oracle manuals. He lived in a second-story apartment with no elevator, telephone, or television. The only way to reach him was to call the neighboring gasoline station. They would call up to him. If the window was open, he came down to answer the phone. Otherwise, forget it.

Genius IT people present many management challenges. They are hard to manage. They are often pulled off to fix things in the systems they previously wrote. They do not easily share knowledge. They do not work in teams well. One of our politically best programmers was Bill. Bill was an average programmer, but he had several useful physical traits. He seldom bathed. His hair looked like he put his finger in an electrical outlet each day. And he had a roving eye — it moved randomly. You could not easily listen to Bill and watch the "eye." But Bill was useful. He was sent to users when they wanted to change requirements. This dampened the waves of change.

LACK OF TEAMWORK

DISCUSSION

On the surface it would appear that teamwork in IT and IT work would occur naturally since the people have a similar focus and similar skills. Contrast this with construction or engineering, where the people have different skill and focus sets. However, in construction it is because of this that sharing of information and some teamwork occurs. Many IT managers pay lip service to teamwork, but then they go out and have people work alone on their tasks. The only time there is teamwork is at a meeting. What a joke! This is not teamwork — just individuals toiling alone.

Why is there not more teamwork? From our experience one reason is expediency. Managers want to get the work done. They perceive that if people work together it will slow things down. Another reason is that in many countries there is a culture factor of the individual over the interests of the group. Trust us, this makes it much more difficult to implement effective teamwork.

So what is teamwork? It is just what it says it is — joint work. When two people work on a task, they have to develop approaches and solutions together. Remember the old saying "Two heads are better than one." Well, it applies here too. Teamwork allows a senior person on a team to delegate some of the routine work to the junior people. Conversely, teamwork allows the junior person to gain knowledge through the experience of the senior person. For these reasons we view teamwork as essential for IT success.

There are several misunderstandings about teamwork in IT. One is that if two people work together, the work is slowed down. If this were the case, then teamwork would be discredited and there would be no project teams. Another misunderstanding is that there is a lack of accountability. When you assign a task to two people, you make one in charge and accountable. A third is that people will be spread too thin. In fact, it is often the opposite. People working together can solve many problems faster and more easily.

In our consulting and management experience, we have found that lack of teamwork is a major cause of problems. However, building teamwork can yield some quick short-term as well as many long-term benefits.

IMPACT

Teamwork is essential for several reasons. First, without effective knowledge sharing, you become overdependent on a few people. Second, it is more difficult to detect problems if people work in isolation. Third, it is easier to grow skills if there is teamwork. Without teamwork there is little backup if someone leaves or is unable to do his or her work. It takes a substantial amount of time and effort for a new person to get proficient with what someone else has done.

Another reason for teamwork is to prevent unpleasant surprises. Suppose a programmer is working alone. He or she may keep the problems to him- or herself. The programmer does not tell management that he or she will be late with the work. The manager assumes things are fine. Then at the last minute the programmer delivers the surprise bad news to the manager. Not good. It happens all of the time. With teamwork, the two people involved in the work discuss it. From experience, it is more likely that awareness of a problem will spread beyond the two people. Moreover, with two people the problem might have a better chance of being solved.

DETECTION

Many IT managers pay lip service to teamwork. But when you look for it, you find none. How do you detect the problem that teamwork is ineffective? First, look at how the IT work is organized. Do the IT managers provide opportunities for the employees to share experiences? Are the project meetings just for status? If the answer is affirmative, then you can conclude that there is little joint effort. Next, observe the IT staff at work. Do you see many instances of people talking together when you visit IT? If not, this is another sign of the problem.

Still another symptom of the problem is that the same programmers and other IT staff make the same mistakes again and again. They perpetually underestimate the same work. They often deal with the same issues. There is no learning curve. The lack of communications and joint work inhibit cumulative improvement and the avoiding of the repetition of problems.

ACTIONS AND PREVENTION

If you find that people are not working together, it is tempting to analyze the situation to determine why this is happening. But often you don't have time to do this. What is a better approach? Implement joint tasks as soon as possible.

Next, provide for sharing of information and knowledge in the IT meetings. As teamwork gets established, hold some meetings where the staff can discuss the benefits of teamwork. This will reinforce the change, help overcome old, ingrained habits, and move the ownership of the idea to the staff. Obviously, you can prevent this issue by establishing and rewarding joint work from the start.

TEAM MEMBERS OR DEPARTMENTS THAT DO NOT GET ALONG WITH ONE ANOTHER

DISCUSSION

Some people see themselves in competition with other IT staff. As such, they do not want to share knowledge. Another factor that contributes to this problem is that through training and culture, the individual is favored over the group. Also, some organizations have no significant turnover of staff. People come in contact and work with each other over many projects and years. For example, at a university with tenure, the same faculty work (or do not work) together for decades. In these situations it is not surprising to find personality conflicts and even hatred.

The project leader often has little choice regarding the team's composition. Managers may assign people to the team. A person may have unique skills or knowledge essential to the project work. This means that the project leader often is forced to take people who have long-standing dislikes for each other going back months and years.

This problem has surfaced many times over the past several decades. In fact, you can almost predict it will happen sooner rather than later. Moreover, the problem is not unique to IT. The employees in two business departments may literally detest each other. This can result from problems between the managers of the groups, the mission and role of the groups, and/or past differences. In one project, which thankfully died, three departments were involved. Each did not get along with the other two. All resisted joint meetings to discuss the project and resolve problems and questions. The project leader attempted to hold single meetings with each group. This proved to be a bad idea. Each user group favored its own approach to problems that, of course, benefited that group. As a result, some problems took a long time to resolve. Other problems were never resolved. When the project leader finally held a joint meeting, there was already too much "bad blood" and distrust. When the backlog of unresolved problems grew too great, management had no choice but to terminate the project. To this day the same departments, even with different people, feel the same way!

IMPACT

It is natural that different departments or individuals may see things from their own perspective. In IT work and projects, life is often a compromise. Whether it involves how transactions are handled, how technical problems are addressed, or the like, compromise and a joint solution are not best, but they are also more likely to result in lasting solutions. One impact of these problems is that solutions reached without compromise often favor one individual or group over another. We have seen that when this occurs, the losing individual or department may not support the decision. Wait, it gets worse. They may try to bring up the issue again from a different perspective — creating more problems in the work.

In a team, the outcome of conflict can be poison to the rest of the team. The problem can grow to the point where people loathe to be in the same room or meeting with the people whom do not get along. This can have a severe negative impact on morale and productivity.

DETECTION

For departments, we have found a useful method to detect problems is to examine specific transactions that cross departments. This should be carried out in the early stages of the work. Here a trick is to act ignorant of the business. Each department can explain how it addresses the work. You can ask simple questions that will highlight the department's attitude toward the work and toward the interfacing departments.

For individuals and departments, a valuable approach is to hold joint meetings early. Here you might present some examples of potential problems that have not yet surfaced. You should then sit back and see what they think. Let people talk as much as they want. Here is another tip: Indicate that you are bringing these things up to establish a joint way of solving problems and issues before the issues or problems become real. Not only do you see how they get along, but you also can determine the extent and depth of the problem — a good early warning of what may be ahead.

ACTIONS AND PREVENTION

When a problem arises, you should not try to ignore it or push it aside. Rather, you should move to a lower level of detail. For business departments this means getting down to the detailed transactions. At that level there is little room for politics or hatred. Instead, there is basic truth. At the lowest levels you will find more agreement than disagreement.

For technical staff, you should pretend or act like you are indifferent and keep asking "Why?" or saying "I do not understand. Help me here." When the technical staff restate their positions at lower levels of detail in nontechnical terms, you tend to find that they have more in common than they think.

Now let us assume that you have inherited work or a project in which the team has become polarized. This is one of the more extreme situations. Can you turn it around? Probably not completely. But you can make the situation better. Here are some guidelines. First, make sure the meetings focus on specific and detailed questions. Then you can employ the earlier suggestions for prevention.

A second step is to assign the investigation of a situation or problem to the two people who do not get along. Schedule another meeting that includes you and the two people. Indicate in this meeting that you realize that there can be different points of view. Next, point out that you are not (we repeat, not) trying to change their interpersonal relations. Rather, you are trying to move the work ahead. We have even stated that "you can still hate each other, as long as the work gets done." This sounds extreme, but it may be the best course of action in the circumstances, since it helps those in conflict to put aside their differences temporarily.

Alternatively, you can try to force them to "bury the hatchet" and be more cooperative with each other. This sounds nice, but it is often impractical because the distrust and negative feelings are very deep and have been long lasting. To summarize, the best approach is to confront the problem by implementing more joint work and effort.

TEAM MEMBERS THAT ARE DIFFICULT TO MANAGE

DISCUSSION

Many people grow up as single children. As such, they did not have to compromise and get along with other kids in the family. As adults this can make them more difficult to manage. Another reason for the problem is that in IT some people have big egos because of their technical knowledge and/or degrees. They think they are "hot stuff." Another reason for this behavior is due to IT managers. The IT managers may tell some persons that their work is critical and that they are the only ones who can do it, making them feel more important. If told this enough times, they really start to believe in their own self-importance. Another reason the problem arises is that such persons may feel they are more valuable than the project leader or manager because they know more.

The issue is not restricted to technical staff. It also occurs with senior users we have labeled king and queen bees. These are individuals who have been in the same job for many years. They believe they have the true path and think they are more important than the project or work. Moreover, they have seen projects come and go many times.

The problem gets worse when managers just accept this as part of management duties and do not attempt to deal with the problem. One of the more extreme instances we have seen was with an employee who, when directed to perform certain tasks, would try to procrastinate or delay the work. This happened repeatedly, even when the work was clearly in the realm of the individual's expertise. It could not be allowed to continue, since the lack of progress was affecting the overall work. We used the techniques discussed in this section. In the end we had to micromanage the person for a while to instill expectations and a new attitude toward work in the project. We did not try to permanently change the person. That would have been impossible. The person was behaving the same way two years later, when we last saw the person.

IMPACT

If people are difficult to manage, they may not take direction well. They may work along at their own pace. To demonstrate their power and the dependence of the work on them, they continue to delay. The end result is that the overall schedule suffers. Another method for these people is just to rush through their work. There may be problems and shortcomings in the quality of the work. This later has to be redone.

In the case of queen and king bees, they may try either to impose their own solutions or steer the work in the direction they desire. Often, this means little resulting change or improvement after the project is completed.

DETECTION

There are several ways to detect this problem. First, you can observe their work and their attitude toward the work. It is important here to observe how they assign priorities among different tasks. When people give your work a lower priority, it reveals that their ranking of work to be done is based on their own feelings.

A second way to detect the problem is to watch if you have to give them the same assignment several times. A variation of this is when they keep coming back with questions about the work. This may indicate that they really do not want to do it.

ACTIONS AND PREVENTION

To prevent the problem, you should give them some small tasks to do at the start of the work. These are typically things that can be done in a few days — certainly no longer than a week. Follow up on these tasks with reviews right after they finish the work. This not only shows them who is in charge, but it also leads to a suitable pattern of behavior for later phases of the work.

When you have identified people who are difficult to manage, do not let up on overseeing their work. Implementing joint tasks between them and others can also help in managing them. Here you are relying on peer pressure to keep them in line.

If you inherit work with people difficult to manage, it is a challenge to turn the situation around. The individuals have already had success with other managers. They may feel that you are just the same. You need to assert your authority early. A good approach is to assign them short-term tasks that you will then closely review. For later work, make sure to divide their tasks in such a way that you review their work every two weeks. These actions show that you are serious about establishing and maintaining your authority as a manager.

WIDE RANGE OF EXPERIENCE AND KNOWLEDGE AMONG TEAM MEMBERS

DISCUSSION

This is to be expected in modern IT work. In the "old days" of IT, most projects were carried out in a specific business department, where people tend to have common experience and knowledge. It is the same with IT itself. When there was only a mainframe-based computer solution and most software was developed, the developers and maintenance staff shared the same skills and tools. There was only one business oriented language — COBOL.

Today, the situation is very different. First, business processes are more integrated and complex. They cross multiple departments. This trend is continuing. For example, in the deployment of RFID in retailing and distribution, you integrate warehousing, logistics, and supplier chain management. Then you can throw in sales and store performance as well.

In IT you now have a mixture of software packages along with locally developed systems. The likelihood is higher that vendors and outsourcing are involved as well. Overall, the situation is more complex and demanding of IT management.

IMPACT

Diversity in skills and knowledge can be a strength, but it can also raise problems. One impact is that it can take longer to iron out questions and situations. This is due to the fact that the managers must ensure that solutions will be supported and implemented by the different people and organizations.

Diversity means that different people may see the same problem totally differently. Here is an example of outsourcing. A firm outsourced a call center to Asia. Service levels were not good. The call center staff could not deal with the diversity of the questions and problems raised by customers. As a result some managers sought to shut down the call center. In handling this problem at least four different solutions surfaced from user and IT managers. The solutions differed wildly from one another. Each manager favored a solution that he or she was comfortable with — standard human nature. In the end, a three-pronged approach was used that embodied several different solutions: (1) improved Website to handle issues without involving the call center; (2) more training and tracking of the call center staff; (3) incentives for good service; (4) customer surveys of work; and (5) establishment of a backup, referral call center in the home country of the firm. As you can see, we used the diverse views to get short-, intermediate-, and longer-term solutions.

DETECTION

Typically, you can detect that there will be diversity when the purpose and scope of the work are defined. Most traditional IT efforts deal only with technical solutions. Today, more and more of the work lies in business change and transition. It is not enough to implement a system. There must be change leading up to and following from the installation of a new system.

More specific steps for detection are to see who can address specific problems that have arisen. Do many of the more complex problems depend on one person? Another sign of the problem is to see what happens if more junior staff attempt to deal with the problems alone, without the help of senior staff.

ACTIONS AND PREVENTION

You cannot really prevent the situation from occurring since it happens often as part of the nature of the work. You do need to recognize the condition and take it into account in planning the work. Greater diversity requires you to spend more time in communications and coordination. Since this activity is already a major part of managing work, some other things will receive less attention. Here a useful approach is to involve users and IT staff more directly in what would be traditional project management. One proven approach is for team members and others involved in the work to define their own tasks and then update their tasks. Another step is more formally to track issues and problems. This will help to ensure that problems do not become more severe.

On the positive side, you might consider holding meetings in which different people share their experiences and knowledge. This can not only facilitate more knowledge sharing, but can also help build a common view of the work.

You should also make management aware of the complexity raised by the diversity. It does not help to just tell them. They may think you are overstating the case. Here is a suggestion: Regularly report on the issues by type and refer back to the scope of the work. Management will gradually see that additional oversight or involvement is needed on issues.

PROJECT OR WORK LEADER WHO IS JUNIOR AND LACKS EXPERIENCE

DISCUSSION

Everyone in a new job starts as a junior person. It has been a curse in many IT groups that people get promoted into project management after having taken just a few basic courses. Then they are left to fend for themselves. The result is often predictable and the same — failure. Either the project fails or a senior person has to be given the project.

Why does this arise? One reason is that some managers place insufficient importance on project management. Another reason is that some larger organizations adopt a standardized method, such as Prince2, PMBOK (project management book of knowledge), or some other method. They think that making such a method standard can make up for or compensate for the lack of experience. This is incorrect. Such methods provide a general framework. However, they do not provide the general how-to techniques that are essential for project management success.

Another factor is that when projects are assigned to one project leader, there is little opportunity or incentive for more senior project leaders to share experience with junior project leaders. There is often no emphasis or push by management for knowledge sharing among project leaders.

IMPACT

There are a number of potential impacts.

• The junior person develops a project plan that is neither realistic nor complete.

• The junior person does not recognize the potential severity and effect of issues that arise in the work.

• A junior person may lack sensitivity and get managers or team members angry.

We all know that undoing a problem that has gotten worse is often much more difficult than solving the problem at the early stages following its discovery. If you have to reassign the project leader, it is often viewed as signs of problems and weakness.

DETECTION

How do you detect if people lack experience? Their resume may look good. They have excellent references. Or, alternatively, they may have been able to work effectively in teams before. None of these is sufficient to indicate that they have the right skills or experience. Here is a guideline we have followed for years.

Until proven otherwise, assume that the person lacks the needed skills or knowledge.

How do you test people's knowledge and skills? One effective way is to pose examples of issues that are likely to be encountered in the work. If they do not respond well, it is an indication that when the real problems appear, there will be substantial issues.

Another method is to probe for their experience in managing work. Have them identify some past work they thought turned out well. Ask what they learned from this experience. What problems did they have to overcome?

ACTIONS AND PREVENTION

The best approach we have found to deal with or prevent this problem is to implement shared project management for all significant projects. Wait! Don't react to this by saying that no one is accountable or that there are insufficient project leaders. We have implemented this solution in very small IT groups. Here are the guidelines for shared project management.

• Identify the person who will be in charge at each stage.

• Have the two project leaders manage several projects at the same time, unless the project is large.

• Rotate project leaders over time so that there is variety and more learning.

- Have the project leaders get together now and then to share experiences
— like sharing experiences over a campfire at the end of the day.

How do you get people to work together in managing projects? First, since you are doing it across the board, they cannot say they have been singled out. Second, you can point out that there is a need to share knowledge. Third, you can get the senior project leader on board by having him or her delegate tasks to the junior project leader.

This approach has a number of benefits. First, the junior project leader learns through apprenticeship. Another benefit is that knowledge is shared. A third advantage is that you will likely get better-quality project management, since different people will have different points of view.

SUBSTANTIAL TURNOVER AMONG TEAM MEMBERS

DISCUSSION

Traditionally, in IT this was viewed as a major problem. It might still be, but you can try to turn it into an opportunity as well. Turnover arises for a number of reasons.

- People are pulled off of the work because of more important or emergency tasks.
- An individual may be promoted or move to another organization.
- There can be instances of illness or personal problems.
- Users may be pulled from a project due to year-end closing, the need to generate reports, etc.

The problem is obviously worse in longer projects. Since many ERP and new systems are major efforts, the problem is probably more common now than in the past.

IMPACT

At first glance the immediate impact of a loss is that the person is unavailable to do the work. Someone else has to be found and probably soon. However, any new person will take time to get up to speed and be effective. Time is needed for socialization into a team. More time is required for learning.

The impacts do not stop there. The team may become demoralized due to the loss. The members may think that the person left because the project was in trouble or not getting anywhere. When management pulls someone out, the team may feel that the project is seen as unimportant.

There is also the loss of knowledge and experience. The American Army experienced this during the Vietnam War, in which new troops replaced existing ones without overlap and sharing of knowledge. Many new troops were casualties. Things did not improve until in later conflicts a policy of overlap was put into place.

DETECTION

You can detect if people are likely to leave by keeping in regular contact. Find out about the range of what they are working on. Another technique is to go to the break rooms or smoking areas and listen to what they are talking about. People generally talk about what they are interested in or what bothers them.

Other, more open signs are the following: A team member is frequently absent from team meetings. The work of a team member is late due to the pressure of other work.

ACTIONS AND PREVENTION

One way to prevent the problem is to implement a different approach for getting people on the team. Traditionally, you would look for the most senior users or IT staff. However, these people will be in the greatest demand and be most likely to be pulled from the work. A better approach is to identify what you require at a minimum. We like to use younger individuals with energy. For IT and users we only want to employ senior people when their skills are required or for specific business rules or situations. This is a more targeted approach to project staffing.

When the project is started, you should assume there will be turnover when you least expect it. Here are some specific guidelines.

- Assign more joint tasks so that work is shared. This mitigates the damage if one person leaves.
- Assign tasks that are two weeks in duration, with milestones. This will limit the damage if someone leaves.
- Have individuals relate their experiences and how and why work was addressed, to share knowledge.

Another technique is to explain at the start that these measures are taken because of inevitable turnover in any project. Warn team members that management has many different and competing priorities, so this project will not have the highest priority at all times. That is part of life.

LACK OF MOTIVATION

DISCUSSION

In business departments can have general motivation problems due to poor management, working conditions, policies, procedures, or other factors. IT can evidence motivation problems if people feel they are stuck in their jobs. They may feel that their work is not that important. It is just a job.

In longer or larger IT efforts you can anticipate morale and motivation issues. It is hard to keep people's morale up in work that seems endless. Having issues unresolved for longer periods of time can also lower motivation. This has been a problem in IT since the 1960s.

IMPACT

Lack of motivation obviously has an impact on productivity. People take longer to do things. Alternatively, they may work on other things that give them more satisfaction. Motivation problems do not go away. This is a recurring problem in longer projects.

DETECTION

You should be on the alert for this issue at all times. Listen to casual conversation before or after meetings, during breaks, etc. Watch body language, and listen to the words used by the individuals.

To test motivation you might want to pose a question or issue and see how people respond. If they show a lack of interest or try to change the subject, you probably have a problem.

ACTIONS AND PREVENTION

At the start of the project, have the team members give you a copy of their resumes. Then have them update these assuming that the project was completed successfully and they did good work. This will help them to define goals in the project and work for themselves. If the project is long, then you can have them update the resumes during the project. This can lead to useful discussions of perspective over the work in total.

Assume that some people will be difficult to motivate. For them you should limit their involvement in the project and work. Getting some new blood onto the project team is a good thing. We have found through the years that many project leaders tend to keep team members in the team longer than needed. Why? Because they feel they may still be needed. They fear changing the team. This approach can lead to morale and motivation problems because these individuals feel they are not accomplishing anything.

NOT MUCH COMMUNICATION AMONG TEAM MEMBERS AND OUTSIDE OF THE TEAM

Discussion

Teamwork in many IT groups is just a word. It is not really implemented. People come together in meetings and relate status and then retreat to their cubicles. There is no real teamwork. Under these circumstances it is not hard to see that there might be little communication among team members. This can happen with users as well, since they may feel isolated from their coworkers by being assigned to the project.

Impact

If people do not communicate, it is more difficult to detect problems and potential issues early. Later discovery means less time to solve the problems. Moreover, the problems may be more severe.

A second impact is that when people work alone and do not communicate, they can struggle with an approach for days or weeks. They may not reveal this to you or others because it might be viewed as a sign of weakness. Overall, we feel from experience but cannot really prove that lack of communication is a major cause of failure.

Detection

See how people interact away from meetings. Wander around and observe, realizing that the process of observation might affect what happens (in physics this is known as the Heisenberg uncertainty principle). To overcome this, carry out unannounced walk-throughs more often.

Actions and Prevention

Here are some specific actions you can take to support more and better communication.

- Devote time in meetings to general, seemingly aimless discussions of work.
- Try to assign several people to investigating a problem or situation.
- Hold some short social get-togethers once a week. A number of technology and manufacturing firms have done this for many years, to good effect.
- Do not cut off discussions. Many project leaders want to follow the agenda slavishly at every meeting. Be more flexible.
- Place greater importance on communication in performance reviews.

NEW TEAM MEMBER HAS TO BE SOCIALIZED INTO THE GROUP

DISCUSSION

You have undoubtedly seen the following: A new person is hired. He or she is introduced in a meeting. Then the new hire seems to disappear — just another body in IT or a user department. Many IT and business managers do give sufficient importance or attention to the introduction of new employees into a group.

IMPACT

The new employee can become isolated and quickly lose motivation. This is the most direct impact. However, other impacts are more severe. First, you have the opportunity cost, in that no one can learn from this new person. Second, the new employee probably learned to do things differently at his or her old firm and may carry over bad habits into the new job. Not good. Carried to the extreme, the effectiveness of the entire group may be less than the sum of the individuals.

DETECTION

This is an easy one to detect. You can visit with the people who were recently hired. Find out what issues and problems they have encountered. How did they get help? If there was no help, what did they do alone?

ACTIONS AND PREVENTION

The first step occurs during interviewing. Indicate how people will be incorporated into the organization. This will set expectations of potential employees.

When they are brought on board, hold a meeting in which the only agenda item is them. Introduce them and then discuss their roles and responsibilities. Next, have them talk about their past job in terms of experience, knowledge, etc. Encourage them to tell stories.

These actions are not enough. You have to follow up with assigning shared tasks. New employees should never work alone. After they have been in the job for several weeks, meet with them to gather their experience. Do the same with existing employees who worked with them.

TEAM MEMBER PERFORMANCE THAT DOES NOT SEEM TO IMPROVE OVER TIME

DISCUSSION

This happens in both business units and IT. Individuals meet a certain standard of performance. Expectations from management are then crystallized. There is little change for many months and years. For years we have had as a goal succession planning to put us out of our current jobs and to get cumulative improvement of employee performance. This sounds good and is, in fact, in many mission or vision statements. It is too bad that there is no follow-through.

IMPACT

If people continue to work at the same level of performance, they may have trouble meeting new challenges that arise in any job. In addition, performance levels may actually start to deteriorate.

DETECTION

One approach is to take a snapshot of employee performance at a detailed level. Do the same 6 months later. Another action is to look in the mirror and ask yourself if you are setting the same expectations. If you do not expect more, many people will not put out the additional effort.

ACTIONS AND PREVENTION

Have as a stated goal in your organization to increase performance and capabilities over time. Earlier, we discussed the use of a resume. Have people take a resume and write down a detailed list of accomplishments and capabilities. Also, if they can, have them indicate when they achieved these things. Every 6 months or annually have them update their resumes. Then they and you can see what the changes have been. As an aside, we have used this approach on ourselves for determining when we were getting stale in a position.

This is still insufficient. You also need to kick off any major project or effort by having team members identify what they hope to gain in expertise from the work. This helps to set detailed expectations.

TOO MUCH TIME SPENT IN MEETINGS

DISCUSSION

In almost all of our positions as managers or staff, meetings have been a curse. Additionally, in our discussion in this chapter we have encouraged more meetings. Meetings take time. They also consume energy. Meetings are obviously essential, but they should be managed.

IMPACT

Many meetings have no defined agendas. In some meetings no one sticks to the agenda. Action items are identified, but then there is no follow-up. The result is that the same topics have to be rehashed in the next meeting. Overall, too many meetings can lead to morale and motivation issues.

DETECTION

Measure your meetings. Keep a log of the use of all conference and meeting rooms. Post on the wall of the department the number of person-hours spent in meetings each week. This will raise the level of awareness of the impact of meetings. It will also show that you are serious about controlling meeting time.

ACTIONS AND PREVENTION

The first guideline to distribute is to have people plan meetings better. They should ask what topics and actions are expected of the meeting. Also, have people ask the following three questions.

- What if the meeting were not held? What would happen? Can some other way be found to accomplish the same thing?
  - What is the minimum number of people needed in the meeting?
  - What if the meeting were deferred for a day or a week?

Convince people that they do not have to be in every meeting. Publish the meeting minutes right after the meeting, and circulate them widely.

Another problem in meetings is that a junior person takes the notes from the meeting. They may get things wrong or generate political problems. Here is a tip: If you attend a meeting, always take the notes. Otherwise, have a senior person take the notes. Here is a basic truth:

Whoever takes the minutes of a meeting controls the truth.

CONCLUSIONS

The approaches that have been identified in this chapter are similar. They focus on more sharing of information, collaboration, and planning. Isolated work and people, whether in IT or business units, tend to generate more problems.

Chapter 5

The Work

INTRODUCTION

In the preceding chapter, some common issues related to personnel and teams were covered. Here we focus on methods and tools and how the work is performed. The types and nature of IT-related methods and tools have changed over the years. Yet experience has shown that many of the same problems remain. Many of the issues mentioned here were uncovered in 1980 in research carried out for software maintenance (see Lientz, B.P. and E.B. Swanson, *Software Maintenance Management*, Reading, Mass.: Addison-Wesley, 1980).

There are some underlying problems in how many IT groups address methods and tools. First, they do not take a systematic approach for identifying, adopting, implementing, enforcing, and supporting them. Second, managers often either too quickly adopt a tool as a panacea or delay adopting methods and tools that are in wide use. The result often is that the method or tool is not properly used. Another problem is that IT managers often do specify their expectations as to what the benefits of the new technique or tool are supposed to deliver. Then the situation gets worse when there is no enforcement of use or setting of standards.

Let's turn to a few definitions. A *method* specifies what is to be done. Project management is a methodology. Using a method by itself without any automated tools can be highly nonproductive. An example was structured programming. COBOL did not easily support it, and, although many IT managers paid it lip service, it was in the end discarded as being unenforceable. The tools were inadequate to support the method. Methods require tools.

On the other hand, some adopt a tool. People are trained in the tool. Then they are expected to use it effectively. Problems arise almost immediately. How the tool is used depends on the individual. For some it works, for others it bombs out. The methods and tools are mutually interdependent. The method should be defined first, followed by the tool.

Even with the "right" or appropriate methods and tools, failure or partial success may occur. Experience reveals that you also need the following supporting elements:

- Guidelines on how to use the methods and tools together
- Collection and organization of improvements in use as experience has been gained
- Definition of the expectations of management as to what benefits employees are to get out of the method or tool
- Identification of an expert who can be called on if questions or problems arise

Overall, the IT organization should conduct a regular, annual review of methods and tools. Such a review should include:

- Potential new methods or tools
- Evaluation of the effectiveness of the current portfolio of methods and tools
- Elimination of methods and tools that are obsolete or inappropriate

Taking a portfolio approach is useful, since the overall situation in methods and tools can be determined. From doing this in over 50 organizations, we have found gaps or holes in any evaluation where there is no endorsed technique or where there is a method but no tool. IT management must work to fill the gaps or at least to develop practices and policies on how the gaps are to be addressed in an organized manner.

LIMITED OR NO GUIDELINES FOR USING METHODS AND TOOLS

DISCUSSION

Let's first take an example. Suppose you have learned project management and are using some standard project management software. If you learned the tool from someone who teaches word processing on one day, spreadsheets on the next, etc., there are some dangers. Your instructor may have had no experience in project management, only with the software. So the person trains you in 350 features of the software over two days. How much of this sticks is questionable at best. Somehow you have to learn from the instructor and then map what you are learning into the context of the method. Is it any surprise that you do not use the tool correctly?

The method specifies what is to be done. The tool helps you do it. However, there is a missing link. That is, you need guidelines on how best to use the tool to carry out the method. Key here is the word *how*.

IMPACT

Without guidelines, six people trying to use the methods and tools will each develop his or her own style. Some might do it well. Many will do it poorly. We have found this to be the case in project management training of thousands of people in over 40 countries. They use the minimum of functions to get by, but they see using the tool as an additional burden.

If different people employ the same tool in a variety of ways, there is inconsistency. Use and effectiveness are uneven. In addition, it is difficult to have the people work successfully together due to this variation. The impact of missing guidelines is lost productivity and more difficult supervision and management.

DETECTION

One approach is to undertake an assessment of the methods and tools that are in place. This begins with a listing of IT activities. Here are some examples.

- Project management
- Requirements gathering
- Design
- Programming
- Data conversion
- Unit testing
- Integration
- Testing
- Training
- System turnover
- Maintenance
- Network management
- Capacity planning
- Security
- Disaster recovery

With this list in hand, you can now identify the methods and tools employed in each area. Even this early in the evaluation you will uncover gaps or missing methods or tools. You will also likely reveal duplicate and overlapping methods and tools.

The next step is to determine if guidelines are available, if there are defined performance measures, if there is enforcement, and if a resource is available that serves as an expert in the area. More gaps will be revealed.

ACTIONS AND PREVENTION

The following problems will have to be faced:

• Old and obsolete methods or tools. Management may be too embarrassed to kill these. But they consume resources and bring discredit on management
• Gaps in the methods, tools, guidelines, performance measures, and experts

Experience shows that it is best to gain agreement among the IT staff that problems exist. If people do not believe there is a problem, they will not want to participate in fixing the problem. Here you can hold meetings and have the technical staff discuss problems and shortcomings with the methods and tools.

Next, you can work to kill off old methods and tools that are obsolete or very seldom used. Experience shows it is best to clean off the plate before filling it up again. After this, you can work to improve how the current methods and tools are used. One action here is to develop among the staff guidelines for better use. Finally, you can start looking for other methods and tools to fill gaps.

TOOLS THAT ARE USED WITH NO STRUCTURED METHODS

DISCUSSION

This issue occurs when management adopts a new tool, such as a programming framework, and then sends programmers off to learn the details of the tool. This sounds like a good approach to get started, but it is fraught with peril. The technical staff will be resistant to change. The staff will have to adapt what they do to the new tool. Some programmers implement systems using the new tool like they programmed 20 years earlier.

The fault for this, if there is fault, is that managers and people in general like to see a new tool as a cure-all for problems. This is not unique to IT or in history. In the early 20th century a Chinese warlord got enthusiastic about Christianity and wanted to make his warriors invincible with the religion. When he asked how to make them change their religion, he was told about baptism. He then used a fire hose as a tool to do this. They actually won a few battles, but they lost the war!

IMPACT

With a new tool, each person who is trained in the tool must make decisions on how to fit the tool into his or her work. Without the structure of a method, each person does this on his or her own. As stated earlier, you first get inconsistent use. Next, people begin to lose faith in the tool. It may become a niche tool. All of the money spent in training could be wasted.

DETECTION

The best and quickest way to analyze the tools is to associate them with methods. When this is done, you will find some tools with only informal methods.

Another approach is to interview several different members of the technical staff to find out what they do and what problems they have. It is likely that a significant number of the problems are traceable to the lack of methods.

ACTIONS AND PREVENTION

You can approach the lack of methods in several ways. If you had a great deal of time, you could start over and define and adopt methods first. Then you could evaluate tools, including those for which you have to determine the goodness of fit with the methods. However, this approach requires the luxury of time. We have very seldom had this. You probably have not either.

A more rapid approach is to see how other firms are using the same tools. Then you can discover what methods they are using. We have no shame. Copy the methods if they fit, in terms of organization size and activities.

If you make changes, do it in one area first. After implementing a new, more formal method, you should then define how the tool is to be used. You will also need to follow this up with reviews to see that it is used. After some period of time and experience, you can hold a meeting to discuss how things are different with a more formalized method. Then you can expand to other areas.

LACK OF FORMAL REVIEWS OF WORK AND TOO MUCH TO REVIEW

DISCUSSION

Everyone feels under time pressure. There is just too much work to do. In a recent survey of over 200 organizations, the authors found that productivity of the IT staff was much less of an issue. The dominant issue was that IT staff was spread too thin.

Given the time pressure, it is not surprising that much of the work in IT and even in the business is not reviewed. Some people depend on problems being noticed later, and then they make an effort to fix the problems — after the fact. So you need to define an approach that selectively determines what is to be reviewed and then find a method for doing the review.

What are some problems with work? Some requirements may not have been met (completeness). There may be too many errors (quality). The work may not be able to be maintained with a reasonable level of effort.

IMPACT

If people know that they will not be reviewed, they may work differently. The most perverse example of this was an aerospace firm that decided to give a big financial reward for documentation of software. Very quickly one of the programmers found that to give the award the company would need an auto-mated way to review and evaluate the code. The number of comment lines was the measurement. So the programmer wrote a routine that generated random characters in lines of comments. For each line of real code, his routine gener-ated 10 lines of garbage comments. He got the award and then promptly left the company and the country. Months later the ruse was discovered.

The lesson learned from this example is that you have to take reviewing work seriously and actually do it — even with the time pressure. Without the reviews there are too many risks, even if everyone is honestly doing his or her work.

DETECTION

A quick way to assess the reviews is to take some sample projects from the past and first uncover problems that surfaced after the work was completed. Then you can trace these back to the development.

Another approach is to look at some of the current work. Here you could ask the project leaders and supervisors how they will review the work. It is useful to ask, "What constitutes unacceptable work?" The answer may surprise you, for they might not have thought about it. A common excuse is that the person

- Determine clearly what the benefits of the method are.
- See how the method is used on work of different size, time, and scope.
- Find out how people have used the method.
- Determine the definition of success in using the method.
- Estimate how much effort is needed in enforcement.

Another step is to determine the goodness of fit between the method and the culture of the organization. Some organizations are very informal and could never successfully implement a formal method.

If you decide to adopt or change a method, work through the implications of the formalization. Ask how people could get around using the method. How would you then detect this? What would be the downside risk if the method is not used?

FAULTY REPORTING ON THE WORK

DISCUSSION

People in IT often report on work in terms of budget versus actual and schedule versus planned effort. This sounds good and seems in line with other business. However, IT is fundamentally different in several respects from construction, engineering, or other work. In standard work, requirements are better defined and more precise. In IT you try to get precise requirements, but often you do not know until much later in the work.

In standard business, the risk or issues tend to be spread across the work. In IT the major risk and issues occur toward the end of the work. There may be problems in data conversion, integration, testing, and user acceptance — all at the end.

IMPACT

If project reporting focuses on the cost and schedule, then managers may think the work is OK, since these two measures do not indicate problems. However, in many IT efforts both of these are trailing indicators. That is, issues and problems worsen while there are no signs of the trouble until it is often too late. Faulty project reporting can give a false sense of security.

DETECTION

If issues surface late and are a surprise, then you have just detected problems in project reporting. Another way to detect potential problems in reporting is to see if management gives attention to work based on the size of the budget, the elapsed time for the schedule, or the number of people involved. Management has only limited time and effort available to track work, so other work that may have more and worse issues goes unnoticed.

As was covered in the first part of the book, management often gives attention to the traditional critical path. Since they have limited time available, the end result can be that they often ignore tasks that have issues and risk.

ACTIONS AND PREVENTION

Guidelines for identifying, tracking, and reporting on issues were discussed in the first part of the book. Here we provide some guidelines for initiating better project reporting. A good initial step is to raise awareness of issues with management. This can make them uneasy, since they thought things were fine. As they see the importance of resolving issues earlier, they will start asking for issues-tracking information along with the standard information.

LACK OF PLANNING FOR THE WORK

DISCUSSION

Suppose you have an experienced team of IT professionals that has done similar work a number of times. One could ask, "Why should time be spent planning the work? Why not get on with the work?" The project or work may be under severe time pressure. Planning time could be spent in work time.

The same could be said for experienced Boy Scouts. What happens when they don't plan? They may forget some items. They may be unprepared for a change in the weather. Some could get sidetracked. There have also been articles about hikers who became lost and suffered from exposure due to lack of planning.

IMPACT

Some of the potential effects of a lack of planning include the following.

• There may not be a common understanding of what work has to be done.

• Without planning, the team members make assumptions about how and what to work on.

• The project leader may also assume that everyone is clear on what has to be done.

DETECTION

When you observe people discussing their work, you can see if they mention past work. If they do, then they become aware of their mistakes. We used to make the same mistakes again and again while traveling. This occurred because we thought that each trip was unique. But that is just not true. When we detected the same mistake for the third time, we decided it was time to take some action. We now keep a list of travel mistakes and review it before each trip. Then after the trip we update our list. It is not pleasant reading, but it does help in preventing repetition of the mistakes.

ACTIONS AND PREVENTION

Use our travel approach to keep a log of mistakes you have made. Divide these up into various areas — work, communication, documentation, planning, etc. Do this especially if you are a manager. This will make you more effective in the future. When you feel comfortable about the mistakes and that you are making progress, you can share them with others. It is always healthy to laugh at yourself now and then.

PEOPLE WHO WORK IN A SINGLE-TASKING MODE

DISCUSSION

Some people appear to be able to work on only one task at a time. This often happens without the person's realizing it. We all get into ruts or behavior patterns that are difficult to break.

Why does this happen when most people can do at least some multitasking? One reason is that they have never been shown any other way. Another reason is that training in school often focuses on completing a task before starting the next one.

The problem in IT is that a lot is going on at the same time. Single-tasking for bank tellers is necessary for productivity. However, the impact in IT can be deadly. If people are hung up on a task because they are waiting for information, then they may not work on anything significant.

IMPACT

A person working in a single-tasking mode tends to be less productive. It takes longer to do the work because the person experiences considerable idle time. If a manager knows that someone is single-task oriented, he or she may only assign one task at a time. This can consume more of the manager's time as well.

DETECTION

Watch how someone does his or her work. You can also infer a great deal by observing his or her workspace and desk. If everything there pertains to one task, then you know that the person is single-tasked focused.

ACTIONS AND PREVENTION

It is not possible to easily train adults to multitask. One method that has worked for us has been to assign to each person several foreground and background tasks — just like an operating system. When the foreground tasks are in a wait state, the employee can work on a background task. Of course, the background task can divert a person from his or her main work. However, this can be introduced judiciously. You can also ask that the individual track both background and foreground tasks.

One benefit of this is that the self-esteem of the individual is improved, since he or she is accomplishing more. Also, the person feels more in control of things if kept productively busy.

CONCLUSIONS

From the viewpoint of self-interest, there is benefit in defining and using as few methods and tools as possible. The constraint here is that the methods and tools must cover the range of IT activities. Experience shows that when there is a gap or no adopted technique, individuals invent their own solutions — impacting productivity and maintainability. Another conclusion is that there should be an adequate infrastructure for methods and tools. This includes guidelines, performance specification, review and/or enforcement, and some sense as to when old techniques might be replaced.

Chapter 6

Business Units

INTRODUCTION

During the entire history of IT, the importance of user and business unit involvement in IT projects and oversight has been widely recognized. Many IT failures have been laid at the feet of the users. Various strategies have been attempted. For some time, users were allowed to go out on their own and acquire services and systems. This was often in response to user complaints that IT was not responsive to their needs. Many of these user efforts failed. Today, things have changed. Business processes cross multiple departments. The processes are more integrated. IT has responded by implementing ERP and other integrated systems.

This chapter examines some of the most common problems and issues associated with users and business units. At the heart of this is the fact that the IT and business unit roles are changing. In the past, individual user departments dictated their own requirements. IT provided systems and services to address these. If you examine multidivision and multidepartment systems, you find that IT has expanded its role from support into coordination. IT does not own processes, but most of the key processes in an organization are not owned by single departments. One emerging issue is the relevance of the current business organization structure. The current organization in many companies is still based on the old "silo" mentality that is over a century old. To see this graphically, consider Wal-Mart's rollout of RFID (radio frequency identification). This is clearly a simple IT project but a complex business project. It crosses logistics, distribution, warehousing, and supplier relations. Who is leading the effort? IT. IT is the only department that spans the organization and provides systems and services. It is hoped that as companies move to the new role of IT, many of the issues in this chapter will lessen or even disappear.

USERS WHO RESIST CHANGE

DISCUSSION

In the past it was often assumed that since management wanted a new system and process, users would endorse the same direction. This is not true. Most lower-level users and supervisors generally are satisfied with what they have. They have been doing the work in the same manner for years. They see no need for change. Change for them represents more toil, sweat, and problems. As such, they see little benefit for themselves in new systems. For example, some ERP implementations require users to input more information for management. This means more work. Yet they are doing the work the same way after implementation.

Resistance to change is complex. First, there are senior users (queen and king bees), who most often do not want change. Second, the users have invested a lot in small spreadsheets, databases, and manual systems (called shadow systems). Third, they generally have a number of problems and issues that cannot be addressed by IT. Yet the only time change occurs is when there is a project to implement new systems.

IMPACT

Users can resist change openly or covertly. Over the years most have found that open resistance is futile. So they often resort to more subtle methods. They deliver requirement changes drop by drop — like water torture. Eventually, IT gives up. Another approach is to get IT to own the project. In that way, they can often avoid being accountable for benefits. Remember that IT by itself cannot deliver benefits unless there is total automation, as in e-business.

The most severe impact is failure of the work or project. Beyond that, there are a number of other significant impacts.

• The system is installed successfully, but the users continue with the old process. There are no benefits.

• The scope creeps and expands so that the project is never finished. There are no benefits.

• The requirements keep changing so that the new system just implements a more modern version of the current process. There are no benefits.

DETECTION

How do you detect user resistance to change? Experience shows that it is best and safest to assume that users will resist change from the start. You can quickly detect resistance during the requirements-gathering and problem-definition work. Simply propose some simple non-IT changes that require no money or major management approval. If they resist or state reservations about even these simple things, then you know there are problems.

Here is an example. We were implementing a new payroll process and system for a transportation agency. We found that all bus drivers had to complete a form at the end of each shift of duty. Since almost all drivers adhered to their assigned times and routes, this form was largely unnecessary. You could make the form exception-based so that only drivers who experienced problems would have to complete the form. The bus drivers loved this. Management embraced it. The payroll clerks resisted. It took three months of political effort to undermine the payroll clerk king and queen bees and get the change in. Unbelievable, you say. Hardly! This happens all the time.

ACTIONS AND PREVENTION

After detecting resistance, you could elect to confront the individuals. In our experience, this has proven to be a bad idea. You merely drive the resistance underground. If you attempt to rationally address their concerns, it will often fail. Why? Because the problem is not business or technical. It is political.

What do you do? Work with younger employees who are more amenable to change. Focus on the common transactions. Do not get buried in exceptions. Use the younger people to bring the resisters along.

To prevent the problem, you should start the life cycle slightly differently. Instead of just gathering requirements, assume there will be resistance to change. First have the employees identify the problems in their work. Then move to determining the impacts of the problems on their work. Here is a basic truth from the area of drug and alcohol abuse:

In order to be cured, you first have to admit you have a problem.

Once people see they have a problem, you can gather requirements and find solutions that address some or all of these problems.

USERS WHO WANT THE TECHNOLOGY BUT DO NOT WANT TO CHANGE

DISCUSSION

Many people like to have modern technology — especially if another department has modern systems. They want it too. Also, most people "want to have their cake and eat it too." It is the same with systems and technology. That is why many systems have been installed that resulted in no change or benefit. But the users got modern PCs and networks. Through excessive e-mailing and Internet surfing, they actually may become less productive!

How do users get ideas about technology? Some are shadow IT people; that is, they work on it at home. They may even consult on the side but work as users during the day. Others have developed shadow systems for their departments. Some managers may attend a meeting, read a magazine on a plane, or somehow find out about some new technology. They may decide it has real business benefits. However, they have not thought through the installation, change, and support requirements. It is amazing how no technology fails in articles that you read at 35,000-foot altitude.

In the early days of digital cameras, a manager at a major insurance firm approached us and requested digital cameras for all of the claims adjusters. They could snap photos, prepare the forms, and submit the whole thing via the Internet. It sounded so simple. However, the resolution of early digital cameras was terrible. In addition, they consumed many batteries. Better to let the technology improve. However, as we will recommend, you can use this as a way to generate a useful project. In this example, we implemented one-hour photo finishing, scanning, and the Internet. The same results were achieved. How did we market this to the managers? First we gave them credit for the idea. Then we indicated that it was important to establish the process first. When digital cameras improved, the managers' solution could be used. They and the adjusters were happy. The problem was solved for two years, by which time digital cameras had improved.

IMPACT

If a user department wants some technology and there is acceptance of this as a project for IT, then there are likely to be many negative impacts. First, there probably will not be any benefits. People will probably blame IT for this. Second, the effort to implement the technology took the already-limited IT resources and stretched them further. Some work that needed to be done had to be postponed.

There may be additional effects. The IT staff may be become demoralized. The entire basis and method of project selection and justification can be called into question.

DETECTION

One sign of the problem is when things have been going along in a user department for some time, but, out of the blue, the manager of the business unit requests some technology. You want to find out the source of the idea. This will give you more information on the motivation. You can carry out the detection work by appearing to be positive on the idea and expressing that you have to gather more information.

ACTIONS AND PREVENTION

Have a standard list of questions ready when anyone proposes new technology. Here is a list we have often employed.

- What is the underlying business problem?
- How could the new technology help to solve the problem?
- If nothing is done, will the business situation get worse?
- If the existing technology and process were modified, would you get the same or a similar result as with the new technology?
- What is the user department willing to do in terms of participation and commitment?
- How will the new technology be integrated into the work and the existing systems and technology?
- What are the support requirements for the new technology?
- Is the new technology easy to use and learn?

When you pose these questions, act ignorant of the business. After all, you are in IT, so you do not have detailed knowledge of the user department. You can state that you have to determine the benefits before anything can be approved.

If the idea is still alive after this, then go into the user department and look for problems. Will or can the new idea be warped or changed to solve a real business problem? If so, you have a winner and you can give credit to the managers and users for coming up with the idea. You can modify the approach for using the technology during implementation.

BUSINESS PROCESSES THAT HAVE TOO MANY EXCEPTIONS

Discussion

Most business processes have exceptions. An exception is created when the existing standard work methods will not deal with a situation. Exceptions can be created by any employee, but they are normally created by supervisors and king and queen bees. What do king and queen bees gain by generating an exception? Obviously, they get the work done. They create an informal rule that similar work will be treated in the same way. The exception requires additional business rules and/or knowledge. The king or queen bee gains more informal power, for when the next exception comes up, they have to be involved.

From this discussion we can see that while exceptions may be needed, they are also political. Power is based in the people who can handle the exceptions. If a department is highly structured and has numerous policies and procedures, then the exceptions are tightly controlled. The same applies to measurement of the work. If the work is closely measured and monitored, then there will be fewer exceptions.

Thus, a process with many exceptions may be deeply in trouble. The wide range of exceptions are just symptoms of the underlying problem of chaos. We find this in some departments when specific employees are assigned to handle a group of exceptions. This sounds more efficient, but it actually creates bottlenecks and uneven work distribution.

Impact

The impact of a faulty business process with many exceptions may first be on user management. Management sees the problem and decides it needs an IT solution. After all, it is politically easier and simpler to call in IT than to try and sort it out yourself.

The next impact falls on IT. Many IT people would take a user request to handle exceptions and start developing requirements, defining business rules, and proceeding with the implementation. Do you see what will happen? IT will automate X exceptions out of $20X$ total exceptions. The users will still have the remainder to do with shadow systems, king and queen bees, etc. There will be no productivity gain. Who will be blamed? IT. Why? IT was supposed to fix the problem.

Detection

When you are asked to respond to a user request, you should visit the area where the work is being done and make a determination about the state of the process. If you find many exceptions, then you have the situation we just discussed.

ACTIONS AND PREVENTION

One way to prevent the problem is to evaluate business processes on a regular basis. In that way, management, IT, and the departments can see where the problems lie. This will head off fixing a bunch of exceptions in a haphazard manner.

You can also structure the user request form so that it calls for more information than the standard form. A standard user request form asks for the problem, solution, benefit, and comments. Our preferred user request form includes the following elements.

- State what the problem is.
- Why did the problem surface now? What has changed?
- If the problem is not solved, what will happen?
- If the problem is deferred, what will happen?
- What are the benefits?
- How would the benefits be validated?
- What is the user willing to do to support the solution?

Now if the problem occurs and you have to respond to the users, you should examine the work and raise questions about the exceptions. Some of the questions we have used in the past include the following.

- How did the exception arise?
- Who can handle the exception?
- If this person is not available, what happens to the work?
- What would happen if the person went away or was permanently unavailable?
- How many of these exceptions occur in a week or month?
- If the exception was handled like normal work, what would happen?

Answering these questions should shake the truth out of the bushes.

MANY SHADOW SYSTEMS IN THE BUSINESS UNITS

DISCUSSION

Related to exceptions and king and queen bees are shadow systems. Recall that a shadow system is either manual or automated, developed within the department, and used frequently. A shadow system may be used by one person or a group. The users highly depend on them to do work efficiently.

Why can't these shadow systems be part of the solution provided by IT? Users may have tried in the past to make requests but been told that IT resources were unavailable. Or the user manager may have decided that approaching IT would be too much trouble or work. Easier and faster to do it yourself, right?

IMPACT

Shadow systems suffer from a number of problems. Here are some of the most common that we have observed.

• The business rules in the shadow system were never tested, verified, or validated.

• The person who developed the shadow system left, and no one knows how to fix it, although they still use it.

• There is no documentation for the shadow system.

• There is no measurement of the effectiveness of the shadow system.

• The one shadow system could not handle all of the situations, so more shadow systems were created.

The users may not think about or even be aware of these problems. They do not realize how vulnerable they are.

If the users rely on the shadow systems a lot, then they may not think much of IT. They see IT as being unable to provide the "real" support that is required. This sours the relationship with IT.

DETECTION

There are several ways to detect the use of shadow systems. If the users make no new requests over a long period of time, then you can begin to infer either that work is very stable in the user department or that the users are making do for themselves.

You should make the effort to visit user departments, even when there is no project or work outstanding. Paying a friendly visit and observing the work can be useful in detecting the shadow systems. Observe also the king and queen bees or anyone who seems to be very busy at their PC. If people are bringing work to them and they keep at the PC, you probably have a shadow system.

ACTIONS AND PREVENTION

Proactively, you can see the extent of the problem by evaluating the business process. This will reveal the range and extent of use of shadow systems. Prevention of more shadow systems is complex. You can give users stories of disasters where the shadow system had bad business rules or was too complex. However, they will still rely on the shadow systems if IT cannot respond.

Assuming that there will be shadow systems, one approach is to get them out in the open. A suggestion from past experience is to provide guidelines on the development, testing, and use of such systems. We think this method is valuable since there are never going to be sufficient IT resources to cover all of the shadow systems.

MANY VARIATIONS IN USE OF THE SAME PROCESS

DISCUSSION

In one case, we observed a 24-hour-a-day banking call center. The management had hired the supervisor from a different bank. They then had allowed each manager to implement his or her own procedures. The end result was a call center doing the same work across three shifts, but with three versions of the process! It was so bad that personnel could not easily move between shifts without major retraining.

Another instance of this occurs in international operations. Each country may adapt a process to fit the culture, language, and local regulations of its area. This can also occur in different franchises of the same firm.

IMPACT

Having a wide variety of versions of a process in use is not a bad thing in itself. The problem comes in the impacts. Customers may believe that they are treated better or get better products at one location than another. IT feels the burden because each business unit or location may want its own system. This has occurred widely in international operations.

When corporate managers attempt to standardize the versions of a process, they often use IT to do it. However, after IT has completed its work, it is possible that the different variations will continue being supported by exceptions, king and queen bees, and shadow systems.

DETECTION

You can visit a location and have people explain how they do their work. Then you can ask about the customers, suppliers, local regulations, language, and culture. How do they handle this? The answers will point to the variations in process.

Transaction: _____

Step	Corporate	Location A	Location B	Location C

Figure 6.1   Transaction Table for Process Variation

ACTIONS AND PREVENTION

The best approach is to anticipate different versions and plan for some variation and how this will be supported. Figure 6.1 presents a table we have used. The rows represent the steps in a transaction. The second column gives the corporate standard. The successive columns give the variation that is acceptable at each location or in each business unit. Of course, you will be able to handle only a limited number of common work processes. This will help structure the variation.

DIFFICULTY GETTING QUALIFIED USERS TO JOIN THE EFFORT

DISCUSSION

In the traditional IT effort, you seek out the most senior, qualified users. After all, they know all of the business rules and have the most experience. But what *do* they know? They know the exceptions and workarounds. They are critical to the operation of the department.

There are several problems with this approach. First, the senior users are the ones that the supervisors and managers most depend on for the work. If they are on the project, the work of the department will most likely suffer. This has happened in the past with many ERP implementations. If the qualified users are assigned to the project, they will most likely be unavailable to work on it.

Another observation is that the less senior employees know only the standard work and business rules but not the exceptions. But why do you want to know all of the exceptions? Because if you automate all of them, you are more likely to implement a new system and process that merely replicates what they have.

IMPACT

The most immediate impact is that you may be inundated by exceptions. This will lengthen the project and bring too much focus on the exceptions. If you gather requirements for five exceptions, why not 10? Why not 100? Where do you draw the line?

The attitude of the department managers and supervisors may turn negative toward IT and the work, since the key people are missing. They see the current work as more important than the project.

DETECTION

Look at the users who are involved in the current projects. How available are they? How much information is being gathered on exceptions? Are they dictating solutions that match what they currently do?

ACTIONS AND PREVENTION

One approach that we have employed for many years is to limit the involvement of senior users. Concentrate on junior users and the common work. Approach the senior users for only specific business rules.

Another guideline is to limit the work devoted to exceptions. If you encounter exceptions, try to get these eliminated rather than including them in the requirements. Track how much time and attention is being given to exceptions.

USERS WHO DO NOT WANT TO ASSUME RESPONSIBILITY

DISCUSSION

Look at the world through the users' eyes. If you were not trained in either IT or process improvement, would you want to accept responsibility for benefits? Hardly. Most users just want to do their jobs. They see nothing in it for them in assuming greater responsibility. They will get no additional money or a reward. On the contrary, they risk being blamed if there is a problem.

IMPACT

If the users do not assume responsibility, what are the consequences? Well, someone has to step up and do the work. Who else but IT, right? That is what happens most of the time. Then what? IT does more of the user work, and then the users disown it. Let's take a mundane example: user procedures and training materials. The users claim they are too busy to create these. So IT staff do it.

But there are problems. First, the documentation involves not the user jargon, but IT terminology. This turns the users off. Second, the user procedures and training materials pertain only to the system, since the IT staff do not know the details of the users' business process. The users do not acquire ownership. The training may fall flat. The users may not use the new system in the way intended. The benefits are not achieved.

DETECTION

You can sometimes detect future problems during requirements gathering. Here is what we do. Uncover some quick-hit changes that can make things easier. Propose these to the users. View their reaction. If they do not embrace the changes, then you have resistance to change and a lack of desire to participate. The same applies if they see no problems in their current work.

Another useful test early in the work is to assign them to carry out some straightforward tasks. How do they respond? If they say they are too busy, then there will be more problems later. If they keep asking more and more questions, they are, perhaps, trying to shift the work to you. Either way, you and they lose.

ACTIONS AND PREVENTION

You can try and prevent the problem at the start, when the work is defined. At that time you can define the roles and responsibilities of the users and IT. Often, the user managers will agree to the roles. But do the managers really mean it? Maybe not. What should you do? Have them show their commitment to the responsibilities by having them assign people and do work. Actions speak a lot louder than words.

If the users are "too busy" or cannot do the work they assumed responsibility for, what do you do? You could fall into the trap of doing it for them. Don't. You will probably fail. Instead, back off and indicate that you cannot do it for them. You may have to play a game of "chicken" and say that the work benefits them and that if they do not want to participate, there will be no benefits. Also, indicate that you have more than enough other work to do. See if this changes their attitude.

If this approach fails, then you have to escalate the issue to management. Indicate that it is not a responsibility issue, but a resource issue. You realize that users are stretched thin, but the work has to continue. Never raise the responsibility issue directly. This can make the manager defensive. It also may give the manager an opportunity to back out of the responsibilities.

USERS WHO DO NOT RESOLVE ISSUES QUICKLY OR ADEQUATELY

Discussion

During work and projects, questions arise that can only be addressed by users. Here are some examples:

- Questions on business rules
- Fuzziness of policies
- Definition of roles of specific job titles in user departments
- A choice between different ways to implement something
- Schedule and work responsibility questions

You might think that most users would be eager to answer questions and solve issues. It is not that simple. There is the underlying power structure in the business unit. Many middle- and lower-level managers are fearful of making decisions because these decisions could be undone later. They would be blamed. So they pass the decision upward.

Users are also busy doing a variety of different things. Deciding on your issue may take a lower priority in the big picture.

Still other user managers may think that the question or issue will go away. It may solve itself. The managers may also feel uncomfortable because they are unfamiliar with the business situation.

Impact

The impact of delayed decisions can be huge. First, work on the project may come to a halt or, at best, slow down. Second, both the users and the IT team members may see a lack of decision making as either indecisiveness or that the work is really viewed as unimportant by user management. Third, morale starts to suffer.

If time continues to pass without a decision, then there will be a tendency to move ahead by assuming some decision. Work then resumes. Days or weeks or even months later a decision is made. What happens if the decision does not fit what was assumed? The direction of the work may change. Some of the work performed after the assumption of the decision may have to be undone or redone.

Detection

You have a number of options here. One is to pose some minor decision questions early and see what happens. If even simple things take time, then you have detected that there will be more major problems later.

Another approach is to frame questions in terms of getting decisions. This will make the communications more formal. It will also help you detect the issue.

ACTIONS AND PREVENTION

To prevent the problem, you would start the work by indicating the need for rapid decisions and the impact on the work of a lack of decision making. You may be met with blank stares and assurances that there will be no problem. Here is what you do. Propose several potential questions and issues. See what they do. These have not occurred yet, but it helps to show the managers what they will be facing.

In the team, you can do a similar thing at the start of the work. Propose several questions and have the team, especially the users, simulate how they would go about making decisions. You want to instill a decision-making process before the questions and issues arise.

USERS WHO DICTATE SOLUTIONS

DISCUSSION

This one is similar to the one earlier issue about the new technology. Here users don't want to discuss problems. They have figured out a solution and now are specifying how you should go about the work.

This situation may arise because the users are quite analytical. They also may have IT expertise and knowledge. They may even have implemented a prototype or shadow system. They know what they want.

Here is an example. In a government agency, the manager, on his own, became interested in Microsoft Access and Visual Basic. He then decided to test his skills by developing a shadow system for the department. He developed and tested the system. He did this right. He trained the users himself. This went well. The people had no choice but to use the system. Later, he found that more work was needed. He did not have anymore time to do it himself, so he called in IT. He explained what was needed and gave IT the code and documentation.

Unfortunately, the solution involved replacing the system with one based in SQL Server and using a thin client. Very different from Access. When presented with this solution, the user manager disowned the entire effort. It died and more shadow systems emerged.

IMPACT

There can be positive and negative possible impacts. On the one hand, if the user supplies a valid solution, it makes life easier. Any car salesperson will tell you that it is easier to sell a vehicle when the customer has sold him- or herself. It is the same here.

The negative impact occurs when the user-supplied solution does not fit the problem. As in the earlier example, different technology may be needed. The problem may be different than what the user thinks it is. There may be wide discrepancies between the time and cost that the user imagines and what is really needed. Explaining this to users may require a lot of technical jargon. This can in turn generate many bad feelings between users and IT. IT is seen as nonresponsive. The users are seen by IT as crazy.

Another negative impact occurs if the solution requires systems and technology with which IT is unfamiliar. If you implement this, then you have yet another technology to support. This happened in the 1980s with some minicomputers. It happens today when a manager wants some odd handheld device.

DETECTION

The main thing to detect is the difference between a problem and a solution. If the user begins with a solution, you should play dumb. Ask what problem is being solved. Keep at it. This will uncover whether the user is only interested in a solution.

ACTIONS AND PREVENTION

It is very difficult to dissuade people who are convinced of the value of their solution. Don't even try. Agree with them, and then indicate that benefits have to be determined. Get down to the detail. Ask how the solution would work in the business processes. Have them give you an example. Ask them to show you why the current solution does not work.

Do not appear negative at the start by raising issues of support, incompatible technology, implementation cost, and effort. IT is already often seen as negative and obstructionist to change. Here is a basic law to follow:

With users and management, never say NO!

Agree, and then in the detail raise as many questions as you like. This is a much better approach politically.

USER MANAGEMENT THAT IS ATTEMPTING TO MANIPULATE IT TO GAIN MORE POWER

DISCUSSION

Can this be done? Does IT offer enough opportunity for a manager to increase his or her power. Yes. This happened and still happens when IT falls under a line manager in the organization. The manager can direct IT to spend most of their resources on his processes. He is guaranteed of great service. The other user departments suffer badly.

What can you get out of IT beside resources? One answer is information from various databases. This can help a manager do more in-depth financial and operational analysis. The manager can then make corrections to increase performance.

There is also negative manipulation. Here the user blames IT for his or her own problems. It is always IT's fault. IT is not responsive. IT did not implement the systems correctly. IT did not meet all of the requirements. IT took too long. The blame list is endless.

IMPACT

The impact of this is to deny service and the same level of service to other groups. The other groups tend to resent not only the manager, but also IT. They may go out on their own. They may complain to management about the level of IT service.

There are also impacts in IT. Because IT feels manipulated, the organization does not trust the manager. This in turn breeds more bad feelings. The problems escalate further.

DETECTION

You can detect this by reviewing the allocation of IT resources to different business units. If a disproportionate share of the IT resources is going to one user, then you have to question why, particularly if the resource imbalance has been going on for some time.

You can also look at the communications relations between IT and the business departments. Do some managers tend to take IT services for granted? If so, this is another sign of the problem.

Another step is to review the nature of user requests to see what information the users want access to. How could this information be used for political advantage?

ACTIONS AND PREVENTION

You might prevent the problem by working one-on-one with each key manager to define the relationship between his or her business unit and IT. Be careful here. Some managers may feel you are trying to get control. Insist that you are trying to be fair.

If a manager is abusing the relationship with IT, you might point out the problems that result with other business units. It is in the manager's own self-interest that the imbalance be redressed.

USERS WHO CHANGE REQUIREMENTS FREQUENTLY

DISCUSSION

This is one of the most common problems cited in the literature. Why does this happen? Many IT people believe that it is just legitimate change. It may be. Things could have changed in the user department and in its processes. However, there are also other reasons.

• The users may not have understood the original requirements.
• The users are shown a prototype or think about the project more and change the requirements. This is natural if you have never seen anything before. What if the only car you ever saw was a tiny one? When you see a large luxury car, your requirements will change.
• The users may seek to change requirements to get the new system and process back to the old system and process. They really like things the way they are.
• The users do not want the new system, so, to delay it, they propose requirement changes.
• A new manager may have come into power in the user department who wants to put his or her fingerprint on the work through changed requirements.

There is also the direct relationship between the elapsed time of the work and the extent of requirement changes. The longer the project goes on, the greater the likelihood of more requirements. That is one of the reasons why longer projects have a higher likelihood of failure.

Some believe that the more complete the requirements gathered from users, the better the system will be. This is not always or even often the case. In fact, if users want to retain the old process, they will create more requirements that will warp the new system back to the old. Consider Figure 6.2, where the horizontal axis is the level of detail in requirements. As you can see, the more requirements you gather, the higher the cost. However, if you gather fewer requirements, then

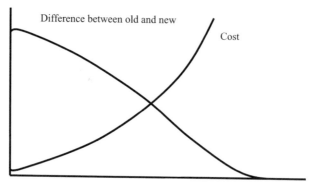
Difference between old and new

Cost

Level of Detail in Requirements

Figure 6.2   Level of Requirements and Cost and Difference

there is a greater difference between the old and new systems. There is greater flexibility and more benefit. Obviously, you need to gather some requirements. The issue is whether you really want to gather an excessive amount.

IMPACT

Getting a few new requirements is probably part of life. However, if there are many changes, then there will a noticeable effect on the schedule and on the cost of the work. The team and in particular IT members may feel that the project is in real trouble. Some may believe it is time to abandon the project.

If this then produces significant delays, there is an impact in the user department. They may think that the project is doomed. They may feel that they will not get what they want.

DETECTION

When you are given a new requirement change, raise the questions in the Actions and Prevention section. This will help you detect whether this is a pattern of change or a single instance. It will also show that you have an organized approach for requirement changes and that you are not surprised. You never, ever want to reveal surprise here because it can be interpreted as a sign of weakness.

Another way to detect potential requirement changes or additions is to visit the business departments on a regular basis. Observe the work. Ask the people doing the work if there is anything new. This accomplishes the goal of an early warning. It also shows the users that you care.

Chapter 7

Management

INTRODUCTION

In our experience, management issues are some of the most common, most complex, and most difficult to deal with. Many IT managers feel a sense of helplessness. This is reasonable, considering that many IT managers have little opportunity for management contacts.

However, many management issues are predictable, given the high management expectations and dependence management feels on IT. Managers often have little knowledge of IT and its activities. Some view IT as a black box. Past efforts over the decades to educate managers in IT have not been very successful. Other managers perceive IT as a barrier or bottleneck to change. With all of this said, you can anticipate a number of the issues that IT managers and staff are likely to face.

MANAGEMENT'S UNREALISTIC EXPECTATIONS OF BENEFITS AND IMPACTS

DISCUSSION

Managers hear about the benefits of IT and systems from a number of sources. One source is the literature, where numerous success stories appear. Some managers do not realize that some of these stories are planted by the vendors of the software. Another source is from vendors and consultants directly. These people want the business and so will obviously play up the benefits of the new systems and technology.

There is a basic paradox here. Management places expectations on IT to deliver benefits and positive impacts. Yet in most organizations, IT has no power or authority to realize the benefits. These depend on the business units. IT can install modern systems completely and perfectly. However, it is up to the users to change their processes and work to take advantage of the new systems.

Why do managers behave this way? Sometimes it is habit. Other times it is the easiest path. It is easier to put pressure on IT than on business managers. The business managers could respond with "It will interfere with the business" or with "If we change, then the business will be negatively impacted. Customer relations could worsen." In several cases, we have observed the business managers actually bring IT managers to the edge of panic.

Impact

One impact of these unrealistic expectations is pressure on IT. This is probably a major source of stress among IT managers. Another impact is that IT then has to press the users to make changes. Users may resent and resist this pressure. The atmosphere between users and IT can become poisoned.

A third impact is back with management. When the expectations are not realized, management often has less faith in IT and what it can accomplish. This can trigger management change in IT. The attitude is "Let's try someone else. Maybe he or she can do better." However, you can change IT managers hundreds of times without affecting the situation. The user and IT roles are the same.

Detection

In conversations with managers, you can detect the problem of expectations by what management says to IT managers and how they say it. If they start the projects with IT, the effect is to place the responsibility with IT. It becomes an IT project. The ensuing problems have already been discussed.

Another way to detect the problem is to observe what happened in past projects and work. If benefits were few, then you have some of the symptoms of the underlying problem of lack of power with IT.

Actions and Prevention

Little can be done to prevent this. You cannot try to educate managers on this. It would fail anyhow. What should you do? Begin by assuming that manag-

ACTIONS AND PREVENTION

There are some preventive steps you can take. First, you can try to maintain informal contacts with upper management. You can provide interesting information in the status reports. What is interesting? Issues that have been handled is one thing. Then management does not have to make decisions. The IT manager seems on top of the situation.

Another step is to keep in regular contact with the business unit managers and outside consultants who have communications with upper management. You have to be careful here, because what you say may be used by them with management.

A third approach is to make IT appear competent but boring. If you get someone excited about something, they will want to get more involved. They might be more inclined to get involved in the decisions. We have employed this method a number of times, and it has worked. In one case we were implementing a new technology. The normal IT manager would show excitement about this to management. We did not because we knew the impact would be more involvement.

SUBSTANTIAL TURNOVER OF MANAGEMENT

DISCUSSION

As one employee in China said to us, "Managers come and go. We are here forever." There is a good lesson to be learned here: The stability of the organization and processes rests with the lower-level employees. You never want to forget this. We never do. While management can initiate work and solve issues now and then, the overall success of a project depends on the people who will do the work and use the system after it is installed.

Management turnover should be anticipated. In one case in doing consulting over several years, there was manager turnover five times. We eventually prepared a package of materials to give to the new manager.

A new manager appears on the scene. What does this person often want to do? Make some changes, have some impact, put his or her mark on the organization. Assume this will occur, and take steps to take advantage of it.

IMPACT

If you do not plan for this, management turnover can be disruptive. You may have to justify all of the projects all over. You may even have to justify your job.

Redirection of IT work by the new manager can be disturbing as well. Some good projects that were making progress may be shelved. This can impact the productivity of the IT group.

DETECTION

If you have a good working relationship with the current manager, he or she may alert you to potential change. Another thing to look for is whether the current manager tends to spend more time away from the organization or business unit. Finally, a third sign is if they delegate more to subordinates and do not appear as interested or involved as they were in the past.

ACTIONS AND PREVENTION

You can prevent problems by taking the following actions.

• Assume that any manager will leave. With this assumption, you should take steps to keep other managers informed as to what is going on.
• Prepare a presentation giving the status of IT work and achievements. Have it ready all of the time. Keep it up to date.

When a new manager arrives, do not wait for him or her to call you. Seize the initiative and call on that person. Provide information on status and achievements. Outline a few potential decisions in which the new manager could play a role with little risk. This may seem defensive, but it is not. You are just trying to get the individual up to speed quickly. We advised an IT manager in Europe to do this. On his own he would have waited for the new manager to contact him. Instead, he showed initiative and established a good first impression. This has worked well. Remember too that first impressions are key.

MANAGEMENT'S PULLING OF RESOURCES FROM SOME IT WORK AND REASSIGNING THEM

DISCUSSION

This can occur due to an emergency. But this is a rare event. Normally, it occurs as part of a management change of direction (discussed earlier in this chapter).

The resources that are extracted may be users or IT people. When this occurs, you might be told that it is temporary. Do not believe it. Temporary things have a tendency to last a long time. Instead, assume that it will be for some time. Plan for this.

IMPACT

If you did not anticipate this, it can be disruptive. Project work is either stopped or substantially slowed down. Then you have to expend effort in finding replacement people. The new people will not have the same skills as the old. Moreover, they will not have the experience of the project or work. The project could even die due to major change.

DETECTION

If a project has high visibility to management, then you can almost expect this to happen. Another case is when the project has team members from users or IT that are very senior and have a great deal of either business or technical knowledge. They are likely to be pulled out.

ACTIONS AND PREVENTION

Here are some useful steps you can take.

• Try to avoid getting senior users or IT staff on your project. In modern IT work, the skills are more widespread than in the past. For the business, the problems of involving king and queen bees have already been discussed.

• If senior people have to be in the work, then take steps to limit their involvement and role. Get them back into their normal work as soon as possible.

• You want to make the work or project seem both important and mundane. If it is seen as important, then they may leave you alone. If the work appears mundane, then they may not show interest in it.

There is another reason that managers pull people out of the work. They may think that progress is insufficient or that the work is no longer strategic in importance. If this occurs, then you made a mistake — a big mistake. You should have detected this earlier and taken action. If the project is a loser, then you want to show initiative by revealing issues and potential solutions.

MANAGEMENT'S ATTEMPTS TO MICROMANAGE THE WORK

DISCUSSION

Why does a manager with many other important things to do attempt to manage projects or work at a detailed level? One reason is that the manager used to be in IT and shows an abnormal interest in IT due to interest and past experience.

Another reason is that the manager believes the project is critical to the organization or his or her own career. The manager may feel that he or she has a great deal riding on the work and thus wants to keep involved.

IMPACT

The direct effect is that the project leader and IT manager lose control. People involved in the project or work do not take them seriously. Instead, they wait for instructions and direction from management. Many in fact like this, since it gives them exposure to managers and a management level that they normally would have little contact with.

DETECTION

If a manager shows an unusual level of interest in the work over some period of time, then you are seeing the early signs of the issue. You can also see it in meetings. The level of detail of the manager's questions can reveal that he or she wants to get more involved in the work.

ACTIONS AND PREVENTION

To prevent the problem, keep the managers informed on a regular basis. Try to make this informal. We have found that one good method is to try and see the managers once a week for 5–10 minutes. Bring her or him up to date on status, interesting events, a story, and even issues. The manager does not have to do anything, and you are not pressing for a decision. The manager may then leave you alone.

Another preventive step is to make the work seem less interesting. If you attempt to get a manager interested, he or she may respond by wanting to get more involved — a bad thing.

- When was the plan last updated?
- Are there specific action items in the plan?
- How many of the action items were implemented?
- Did the project ideas in the plan turn into projects?
- How much of the current work in IT does not fit within the plan?
- Do the action items and project ideas in the plan support key business processes?
- Does the plan contain a link between IT objectives and key processes?
- Does the plan contain connections between IT objectives and strategies on the one hand and the business mission and vision on the other?
- How many people in IT are aware of the plan?
- Is there a proactive strategic resource allocation method that uses the plan?
- Is there an effort to map the elements of the IT plan to specific business units?
- In the review of new project ideas, is there a process to see how the idea aligns to the plan?

Figure 7.1   Checklist for IT Planning and Plan Effectiveness

list of items to help you evaluate how the plan and planning are used. If the answers to a number of the questions are negative, then you can reasonably infer that the plan does not mean much.

ACTIONS AND PREVENTION

If there is no plan, then you can take steps to create one fairly quickly. Space does not permit us to give you the details here. However, a pragmatic approach is given in an earlier book, *Manage IT as a Business* (Lientz and Larssen, Butterworth Heinemann, 2004).

If a plan exists but is not being used, then you can review the plan and extract out of it lists of IT objectives, strategies, issues, and action items. You can resurrect the plan by relating these planning elements to key processes. This is done through tables such as:

- IT objectives versus processes — the benefits to the processes from achieving the objectives
- IT action items versus processes — the impact of the actions on the processes
- IT issues versus processes — the negative effect of not solving the issues on the work

Next, turn to the action items and determine which of these were implemented. What was the result.

LACK OF ALIGNMENT OF IT TO THE BUSINESS

DISCUSSION

Alignment of IT to the business has been a hot topic for some time. The concern from a management perspective is that IT is doing tactical support work when it should be more strategic. In short, managers may perceive that IT is working on useful but not valuable things.

Some technical managers have difficulty with discussing or dealing with alignment. It appears to them to be fuzzy. After all, they think their work is of value and that they are contributing to the business. The alignment, they may feel, is obvious.

Unfortunately, you can never assume that managers think that IT is aligned to the business. It is safer to assume the opposite. Thus, alignment must constantly be demonstrated. In that way the issue of nonalignment has less likelihood of coming up.

Lack of alignment may stem from the IT group's being involved only in tactical work and support. Why does this happen? Some IT managers are risk aversive. If they take on a big, more strategic project, there may be a higher risk of failure. They may prefer to play it safe.

IMPACT

If management perceives a lack of alignment or thinks there really is a problem, then managers may take steps to improve alignment. These steps are not typically pleasant. The IT manager may be replaced. Consultants may be called in to oversee IT. The manager may attempt to micromanage IT.

DETECTION

Look at the mix of the current workload in IT. How much is routine support versus projects? If most is support, then there is an alignment issue, because only very limited resources are going into efforts to improve the business processes.

Another sign of problems is to examine the projects. Are most of them generated reactively from single departments? If so, then IT projects are tactical and not strategic. You could do a million of these and there would be long-term strategic impact on the business or the achievement of the vision of the organization.

ACTIONS AND PREVENTION

The first actions to take involve evaluating the current work. Here are some specific tables to prepare.

• *Projects versus key processes.* Here the entry is an X if the project supports the process. It is blank otherwise. Infrastructure projects, for example, tend to have many X's. Look for a row in the table that has no X's. This is a project that is tactical and is supporting no key project. Maybe it should be killed. Now look for an empty column. This is a process with no project. Either the process is perfect and needs no project (highly unlikely) or it represents an opportunity for a new project.

• *Resources versus projects and support.* Here you list the IT staff as rows and the areas of support and projects as columns. You can now put a rough percentage of time that they spend in each area in the table. If you add this up and normalize it, you can see the distribution of resources between projects and support.

• *Resources versus business units.* This is similar to the preceding table. This table can reveal the distribution of staff resources among business units.

From measurement, now you can turn to actions. One initial action is to kill or reduce the resources in marginal projects. Another action is to examine the resources expended in support. Many IT people prefer doing support over projects. It is less demanding and less stressful. Try to control the time in support. These actions can provide resources for initiating new projects or work that is more strategic.

CONCLUSIONS

Many IT managers feel somewhat helpless with management issues. This is natural since they believe they have no control over them. However, this does not mean that you can do nothing. For each of the issues discussed in this chapter, there are specific actions and steps that can be taken to increase the effectiveness in dealing with management issues.

Chapter 8

Projects

INTRODUCTION

Project management has been around a long time. Methods and tools have come and gone. However, the issues presented here go back many years. They remain as a constant reminder that project management issues involve management and people — often more than they involve the technology and systems.

More specifically, the issues presented here can be traced back to the early 1960s, when one of us started in IT. We have a closet that contains old project files. These files, some of which are over 40 years old, contain the same issues.

PROJECTS THAT DO NOT SEEM TO START OUT RIGHT

Discussion

Haven't you seen this before? A project seems to get going in the right direction. Then many issues appear. People have different ideas of what to do. The project may get sidetracked into other, unplanned areas. A reason for this is lack of planning.

The problem often lies in lack of structure at the start. Someone comes up with a project idea. It is approved without a great deal of discussion and analysis. People figure that the details can be sorted out later when the project plan is reviewed. A project leader is appointed and creates a project plan. If the project leader is typical, this will be a plan that has quite a bit of detail. The problems have begun. The project leader had to make assumptions in order to create the plan. Things are starting to unravel.

When the plan is reviewed, managers raise questions, but they may be intimidated by the detail. They do not want to see the plan again. They figure they can correct problems later. Things are really going downhill and no one seems aware of it. On the surface everything is fine.

IMPACT

The impact of the problem is that additional work has to be expended to get the project back on course. This can take as much effort as turning a steamship or cruise ship. Turning a project is not like paddling a canoe.

The morale of the team is impacted. People on the team now feel that what they did was worthless. They have to do more work, but the schedule allowed for the work did not change. What is worse politically is that team members now begin to feel that management does not know what they want. They begin to mistrust both the project leader and management. All of these are clear signs of future failure.

DETECTION

You can detect the issue by asking the team members individually what they feel the purpose and scope of the project is. Do this with management and the project leader. You may find as many different views as there are people.

Next, look at the project plan. If the task wording appears vague and could fit any number of other projects, then you have ambiguity. Ambiguity and fuzziness in a project plan are normally not desirable. Some vagueness is useful for political reasons, but a great deal of it presents a problem.

ACTIONS AND PREVENTION

How can you prevent this problem? At the start of any project, insist that a project concept be developed. The project concept should contain the following elements:

- Purposes of the work — technical, business, political, cultural
- Scope of the work
- Likely issues to be encountered
- Roles and responsibilities in the project

- General schedule for the work
- Impact on the business if the project fails or is stopped

Why is this a good idea? Because it helps people to develop a common vision of the project and work. It has been shown to prevent later scope creep and requirement changes as well. Moreover, it is politically useful. Why? Because the work has not started yet. There is no plan. Managers can argue over purpose, scope, and roles at little or no cost or effort. Talk is cheap here. It gets expensive later.

You can also use the project concept if you detect the problem in a project that has already begun. Do not stop the work. Go back and gather people to develop the concept. To speed this up, you can define a strawman or candidate project concept and get them to review it.

TOO MANY SURPRISES IN THE PROJECT

DISCUSSION

What is a surprise? Some unexpected or unanticipated event. A surprise, whether unpleasant or pleasant, catches you off guard. You are not prepared for it. Now, your personal life may bring many nice surprises of which you have fond memories: Someone asks you out for a date; you get a present you did not expect; a surprise party is thrown in your honor. This is not so in projects.

Project management related to IT can also harbor surprises. Sadly, experience tells us that many of these are not pleasant. When a user manager calls you up or comes into your office, it is usually not to say that you are doing a good job. He or she is there about a problem or a request.

Why does this happen? Some surprises occur because of the nature of IT. IT, like a fire department, is a service organization. Both respond to problems.

Many people think that surprises cannot be controlled, that they just happen. This used to be the case for fire departments. Then fire departments started implementing a policy of inspecting buildings to help prevent fires. The number of surprises for them dropped. There are steps that can be taken to prevent and mitigate surprises in IT work.

IMPACT

What is the impact of a surprise? What you are working on is disturbed. The surprise takes time to deal with. There is additional stress. After you deal with the surprise, it will take more time to get the work back on track.

Politically, there are more impacts. When caught off guard, some people act defensively. Their attitudes and demeanor do not come off well. This often can make a negative impression. It will take time to reverse this politically. And you probably know that the person who surprised you will always remember your initial reaction, like a deer caught in the headlights of a car.

If others are aware that you were surprised, there could be more problems. Managers may think that you should have been more on top of the work. They may question your management abilities.

DETECTION

You can detect if you are having problems with surprises if you record and track the frequency, subject, and nature of each surprise. This is one action item you can take now.

If you find that surprises are more frequent, it can mean several things.

• You are overfocused on the work and not getting out and communicating.

• You are not as aware of what is going on around you as you once were.

• The problems are building up and you have been unable to deal with them successfully.

ACTIONS AND PREVENTION

In addition to the action on tracking, you can prevent surprises by staying in touch with people. Here are some specific steps.

• See managers on a regular basis. Do this informally. Politically, this is good for you. It shows that you care for the services you provide to them. Also, you will get an early warning of an issue. Third, you do not show up with a problem yourself, so the managers are generally happy to see you.

• Go around IT and talk to the staff about what is going on. See what they are working on. Volunteer to assist. This helps politically and provides you with more information.

• Keep a record of contacts you have made each week. Plan ahead for the next week. Try to see key managers at least once every two weeks.

These suggestions make sense. They are simple to do. Why don't people follow them? They take time, and time is a precious asset in IT — actually, the dearest asset. Also, this takes initiative and requires a person to be outgoing. Some IT managers are not outgoing.

You should also expect surprises. Be ready at any time to give status to and address active, open issues. It is similar to what the old television show *Candid Camera* used to say: "When you least expect it . . ."

After you have experienced a surprise, look for a pattern and analyze the surprise. Here are some questions to answer.

- Was there a political motive in the mind of the person who came to you?
- Could the person have waited?
- Was the situation that urgent?
- When was the last time you were in contact with this person?
- Could you have anticipated the surprise?

TOO MUCH UNPLANNED WORK IN THE PROJECT

DISCUSSION

Every project has unplanned work — things come up and you have to address them. This becomes a problem only when the amount of unplanned work and effort is great. This can be a symptom of a number of different problems, including the following.

- The scope of the project is expanding.
- The original estimate and planning for the work are faulty.
- There are new requirements within the existing scope.
- Users or managers are trying to use the project to get other things done.
- The team members are using the project to get other things done.

IMPACT

Unplanned work was not in the schedule or plan. That is obvious. So that means that unless the team works with abnormal energy and effort, the schedule will slip.

Another impact is that you now do not know how much of this is going on. In the worst case, you might have an "iceberg project," in which a high percentage of the work is unplanned. This is not a good sign. In fact, it's an omen for failure.

DETECTION

It is best to assume that unplanned work is going on. That way, you will not experience a surprise (addressed earlier). What should you do? Visit the team members twice a week and find out what they are working on. Ask them if there is anything new. Is any work taking longer than estimated? Then you can get at the source of the extra work and slippage.

ACTIONS AND PREVENTION

You can begin to prevent it at the start of the project when you establish the scope. Validate the scope of the work in the business process or situation. Next, when you have requirements, validate them with the process.

During the work, assume the worst. New requirements and changes are occurring. Visit user departments on a regular basis to both detect and deal with these things.

Another action is to impose a rule on the project team: Team members have to come to you if they find any unplanned work of more than two hours. This may seem stringent and tight. Don't worry. Start with this, and later you can relax it to a day. The political point here is that you want the team members to know that you are taking unplanned work seriously.

Now turn to the actual work. Insist that users go through the project leader with any changes or requests. They are not to go to team members. Each change will be viewed in light of the questions we raised earlier about new requests and requirement changes.

DIFFICULTY MANAGING AND TRACKING MULTIPLE PROJECTS

DISCUSSION

Different projects involve different users, project leaders, and schedules. If you leave the setup and management to the project leaders, then each project leader will develop a schedule based on his or her own style and experience. Thus, you could have the same work with five different project leaders and end up with widely varying project plans in terms of detail, milestones, and identification of risk.

Now look at what is common to the projects. In general they share the same pool of resources. They share the same issues. The underlying project management methods and tools are the same.

The problem often arises because management sees neither the need for more structure across the projects nor the urgency. This happened in an outsourcing software development firm in Asia. Each project manager did his or her own thing. Some used spreadsheets for project tracking. One used Microsoft Outlook. Others employed Microsoft Project. You could not put the schedules together.

IMPACT

If there is no organized approach and structure for the projects, then you cannot roll up the schedules to get an overall view of the work. What are you missing out on? Here are some answers.

- Most IT managers and general managers like to see a GANTT chart that summarizes all projects. They can compare the progress of one to another. This can also generate a sense of calm.
- Resource management has been a key theme throughout the book. It is difficult to get a picture of what resources are required across the projects.
- Issues cross projects. If the projects were organized and relied on the same master list of issues, then you could easily see those issues and their impacts across the projects.

There is another political impact: If management does not impose structure and more uniformity, then the IT staff and project leaders are more likely to believe in the uniqueness of each project. It is more complex and harder to gather lessons learned across the work.

DETECTION

It is easy to detect when there is a lack of structure. Just ask the project leaders for their plans. If you get different approaches from each project leader, then you know this problem exists.

Another sign of the problem appears if management deals with one project at a time. Each meeting focuses on a single project. The issues are always project specific.

ACTIONS AND PREVENTION

The beginning of the effort to impose structure starts by showing the project leaders that they are doing extra work because of a lack of structure. We have carried work to implement structure in managing projects many times. A basic lesson learned is that until the IT project leaders and staff realize the benefits from organization and the problems with "going it alone," there is little hope of lasting change.

The next steps are to identify a common list of issues and to define project templates for the work. A template is a high-level plan with dependencies but no durations or real resources. You can use a template to generate a plan. This saves time, improves consistency, and supports multiple-project analysis. The templates are stable and can improve in detail over time with experience.

The templates are modular. You can have templates for data conversion, testing, development, software acquisition, etc. The overall plan is composed of separate but interrelated templates and plans. This is a component-based approach.

After this you can carry it further. You could impose even more standardization. You could deploy Prince 2, PMBOK (the project management book of knowledge), or some other method.

TIME-CONSUMING PROJECT ADMINISTRATION

DISCUSSION

In traditional project management, such as construction, a project leader spends a great deal of time and effort in project administration. This includes working with the project management software, entering and updating task information, tracking project status, and doing project reporting. Individuals in the project management office spend most of their time doing these tasks.

IMPACT

We have already shown in IT that projects are different. You need a more collaborative effort. If the project leader spends all or most of his or her time in project administration, the leader becomes detached from the work. He or she may be obsessed with either accuracy or detail or both. This means that the leader has less time to deal with issues and no time to perform actual work on the project.

The team feels effects as well. Because the team members did not define their tasks and do not update them, they have no sense of ownership of the plan. It is the project leader's plan. Certainly, it is not their plan. This creates problems and misunderstandings later on. It gives the team members an excuse when problems arise. The underlying problem is that the people doing the work are best suited to defining their own detailed tasks.

DETECTION

Observe how several project leaders spend their time. Are they out with IT staff, vendors, management, and users? Or are they working at their desks using their PCs all day long? If so, you definitely have a problem here.

Next, see how issues are addressed. Are the project leaders aware of the details of issues? Or are they familiar with issues at a more general level? If the project leader appears detached from the issues, this could spell doom or at least future major problems.

ACTIONS AND PREVENTION

IT managers sometimes have no expectations or goals with respect to the time management for project leaders. Here is a mix that we have found desirable, even if it cannot easily be achieved.

- Addressing issues — 40–50% of time
- Communications — 30–40% of time
- Project administration — 10–20% of time
- Doing work in the project — 10% of time

You may never get there, but in pursuing the goal you will reduce the percentage in project administration.

How do you proceed to reduce project administration time? Here are some specific guidelines.

- Adjust the frequency of project meetings to match the number of issues. When there are few burning project issues, you can hold fewer meetings. Fewer meetings equals higher productivity.
- Have the team members define and update their own tasks. The project leader can then review these and the updates. This gets the team members involved in the project management of the work.
- Standardize project reporting so as to make this easier.
- Have all formal presentations structured into the same outlines. This saves time.
- Reduce the number of formal presentations and focus instead on informal communications. This saves preparation time.

PROJECT LEADERS WHO LACK SKILLS AND KNOWLEDGE

DISCUSSION

How do people become project leaders or IT supervisors? Often it is not due to their skills or experience. It may be the people are doing critical work and are at the top of their salary range in their current job. To keep them and get them more money, you move them into a management position.

Most organizations lack a structured approach for grooming people to be good project leaders. They may send them to a few seminars and have them read a book or two. IT management is sometimes at fault, because they think that the most important attribute for project leadership is technical knowledge. This fails. The key critical success factors in IT project management are problem solving and communications. A technically oriented project leader may try to do the work herself or himself. She or he will micromanage the team or downplay management issues and concentrate on technical issues. All of these create many problems.

Impact

Untrained project leaders tend to make many mistakes. Moreover, they will probably not learn from the mistakes quickly. They may have no examples of successful role models. They do not acquire knowledge from others.

For IT, overall this creates other, more severe problems. The IT managers may have to devote more time to the junior project leaders. They assign the junior project leaders to less risky work. What is the impact of this action? The burden of the risky work falls on the very few experienced project leaders.

If this continues, nothing gets better. There is no improvement. Things just get worse. The experienced project leaders get burned out. The junior ones continue to wander aimlessly in the forest. This is not a pretty picture.

Detection

Just look at the last appointed project leader. If this person was promoted from a technical job, find out how he or she learned project management. Look at the samples of this individual's plans and status reports.

Another way to detect the problem is to attend some project meetings where multiple project leaders are present. To what extent do the different project leaders interact? If not much, this is a sign of trouble.

Actions and Prevention

Actions and prevention begin when people are named to be project leaders. You should assume that they have limited project management experience. Assign them to work with another, more senior project leader. In effect they become an apprentice to the senior person.

The general policy to consider adopting is that every significant project should have two project leaders. At any time, one of them is in charge. This yields a number of benefits.

- Junior project leaders improve their skills and knowledge.
- You have some degree of backup if one of the project leaders leaves. If you have only one project leader and that person leaves, you may be in deep trouble and it may take a long time to recover.
- For every project issue, two people now consider, examine, and analyze the issues. Two sets of eyes are better than one.
- With users and vendors, they can play good cop, bad cop. That is, one can be friendly and the other hostile. If you have one project leader who attempts to play both roles in a meeting, that person may appear slightly insane.

How do you get senior project leaders to agree to this? They may think that it will slow them down or that they will be less productive. Point out that there are a lot of routine things that the junior person can do. This frees up the senior project leader for more interesting work.

We have implemented this approach in very small IT groups. It works for the reasons just cited. It is not more work; it is different work.

Here is another tip: Rotate project leaders so that they get to work with different people. This will help share the skills and knowledge.

LACK OF STANDARD PROJECT REPORTING

DISCUSSION

You may have standard reporting for larger projects. The issue is what is done with the smaller projects. Imposing a major reporting burden on these could produce substantial, negative impacts. One is that because people see the burden, they try to avoid calling the work a project. This means that small projects are managed like routine support. They are less controlled. A second problem is that the borderline between large and small is fuzzy. As a result, even medium-size projects try not to be projects.

IMPACT

Some of the negative effects have been discussed in the preceding section. Another impact is that each project reports differently. There is no consistency. It takes more time for management to determine what is going on, what items need more attention, etc.

When there is a lack of structure, each project leader invents his or her own reporting approach, usually based on the individual's project management expertise and opinions. Some leaders, for example, may not want to share information. They provide the minimum amount of information. As you are aware, this can create major problems later.

DETECTION

Look at how project reporting is done now. You should give special attention to smaller projects. Examine how management determines how work is labeled a project.

Now look at the project reporting that is being done. Obviously, it contains status on the schedule and budget. However, as was pointed out earlier in the book, these are trailing indicators. A key is the information provided on issues. At a minimum there should be the following:

- Indication of the status of the major, outstanding issues
- Identification of new issues
- The extent of future work that has issues
- Expected, potential issues in future work
- The amount of the previous work that had issues

This will give you a better handle on risk and issues.

ACTIONS AND PREVENTION

Let's take the suggestions in the previous section and make them more formal. In Chapter 2 you have the guidelines for more effective project reporting.

How do you get management and staff in IT to adopt this more structured approach? After all, they may resist it. Here are some of the excuses we have heard.

- What we do now is OK.
- It has worked in the past, so why not continue?
- It will be too much work to report more information.

What is behind the resistance? Old habits is one factor. Another may be information hiding; people may not want to share information.

How do you deal with this? Point out how unpleasant surprises with issues could have been avoided earlier through issue detection. Another step is to give an example of a project that seemed OK using standard measurements but was in deep trouble on issues.

What are the effects? Morale drops as the staff become overwhelmed. Quality of work can plummet as the staff just try to get stuff done. The thought of doing excellent or even good work goes out the window. Another effect is that many projects collectively raise user and management expectations. Each project has a set of users. They have specific expectations from the project. More projects translates into more expectations. Eventually, the workload breaks the back and will of the people doing the work. Then a crisis occurs and ad hoc emergency measures are taken. This is akin to jettisoning everything to make a boat or plane lighter.

DETECTION

This problem can be observed in a number of ways. You can see what individual people in IT are working on. You can observe what they are actually finishing and accomplishing.

Another approach is to compare the number of projects started to the number completed. If new projects keep arriving and projects are not finished, then you know that this issue is alive and well.

ACTIONS AND PREVENTION

A number of actions can be taken to both prevent and address the issue. First, you can modify how new project ideas are examined and how projects are selected. Use the project concept discussed earlier.

Another step is to do strategic resource allocation every three months. Here management review the progress of existing work and new project ideas that have survived the filter of the project concept. Instead of looking at the projects, concentrate your attention on the resources. Answer the following question: How can the resources be best deployed over the next quarter?

This method provides a more systematic way to manage projects. You can kill some projects by putting them to sleep. You can admit new projects so that management sees that IT is more responsive to management needs. Finally, the approach places more pressure on the project teams to deliver results. This is particularly useful in longer projects.

NOT KNOWING WHAT IS GOING ON IN THE PROJECT

DISCUSSION

You have the status of the projects. Isn't this sufficient? If the projects appear to be on track, then there are no issues. Right? Wrong. You need to validate that the status being reported is the real status.

IMPACT

If you do not validate the status of the work, you could find yourself responding to one unpleasant surprise after another. You are being governed by emergencies. You and the organization are losing effectiveness.

DETECTION

If a number of bad events were unforeseen in the status reports, you know that the issue is present. Another thing to look for is the management of issues. If the issues arise and are not linked to the status of the work, this is a sure sign of problems.

ACTIONS AND PREVENTION

The best action is regularly to focus on one project and determine the true state of the work. Here are some specific actions to take.

• Go to the people doing the work and find out what is going on. Does this match the plan? Is there additional work that is not in the plan? Are people spending more time than estimated on other work?
• Map the issues to the tasks in the plan. Is sufficient attention being given to the tasks corresponding to immediate, pressing issues?

CONCLUSIONS

Since these issues tend to recur, you should treat them as part of project management. They are ongoing, since, if you solve all of them at one time, they can reemerge months or weeks later.

How project leaders deal with the issues in this chapter has proven to be a good test of their effectiveness. You might use this, as we have, as a tool in evaluating the project leaders.

Chapter 9

Resistance to Change

INTRODUCTION

Resistance to change in general was discussed earlier. The IT and business managers have to assume as a precaution that there will be resistance to change, for the many reasons we covered earlier. In this chapter we examine some of the reasons that people give for not wanting to change.

At a major petroleum-energy firm we had to implement change in the way projects were managed and planning was performed. We encountered resistance from engineers, managers, and geologists, even after management had dictated that the new approach be followed and after a pilot effort had shown the benefits. The same reasons were often given for not adopting the new method.

Out of frustration we identified 35 reasons to resist change. After analyzing these and determining how we would respond, the reasons were numbered. In the next meeting someone raised one of the reasons. Ah, we responded, "That is number 15." The person was stunned. Then we showed him the list along with our responses. That effectively ended the resistance, just like the Borg in *Star Trek* who said, "Resistance is futile. You will be assimilated" (joke). Since this engagement, we have employed the list repeatedly. It helps to get IT and management ready for resistance. And when you are better prepared, it is easier to overcome the resistance. This chapter contains some of the most commonly encountered reasons that people give.

CHANGE THAT DOES NOT FIT OUR WORK

DISCUSSION

People are comfortable in how they perform their work. They have done it this way for years. Now a new system comes along and they have to change.

Immediately they think that they do not want to change. They grasp for reasons why they cannot change. A good candidate is that the change from the new system does not fit how the work is done.

This reason may, in fact, be valid in some cases. There have been instances in which requirements were gathered from only a few senior users, with no effort to validate the requirements since IT trusted these users. Work progressed. The system was developed and tested. Then came the training. Surprise! The employees started to bring up examples of work that the system could not handle. Some of these transactions were higher-volume work. The IT group was victimized by those few key users. The system had to be modified. Parts had to be redone. There was a four-month delay. What happened to the king and queen bees who gave the wrong information? Nothing. They just returned to their work.

Another reason that the change does not fit is that the business process changed after the requirements were defined. This is less common, since many processes are relatively stable and the elapsed time between requirements and deployment was limited. It is more of an issue when the elapsed time is long.

IMPACT

If the change does not fit the work, then something has to give. You have to either modify the system or change to fit the work. Or, alternatively, you have to change the process to fit the new system. We already discussed the first case. In the second case this is often the purpose of installing the new system and process. You want to get change.

For example, it is not often the case that an ERP system easily fits in with the current processes and practices in an organization. A number of informal processes may be going on in addition to formal processes. The ERP system, if successfully implemented, changes this by imposing more structure on the work.

DETECTION

In order to detect if there will be problems, you should go out and validate the requirements during the work. Look for any changes in the work. This will also keep the IT group in touch with the users.

Now turn to IT. The problem is sometimes that what was stated in the requirements and the design is not carried out in the final product. Have you ever gone to an auto show and seen a prototype car that you immediately liked? Then you find out that the manufacturer is going to put it into production. You get really excited. When it comes out, you cannot wait to get to the auto dealer to see the car. Then you see it, and you say, "This is not the same car." Right.

DETECTION

Detection of the problem begins with observing how the project team goes about their work. If they do not think about the employees or consider the additional work, then you know that problems are coming.

You can also see the problem in action when the system is rolled out and training is done. If the training and rollout do not address the additional work overtly, then there will be problems later.

ACTIONS AND PREVENTION

The best action here is prevention. When you gather requirements for a major system such as an ERP, you know that additional information will be needed. Knowing this, what should you do? Identify the problems that the users have. Many of these will have nothing to do with IT or systems. But they are important to the employees and have not been addressed.

Let's give an example. In implementing a manufacturing system, we found that the evening shift ate their lunch in the middle of the night on the floor of the factory. The factory was in an unsafe area, and people left with security escorts. We asked why they were not given tables and chairs. They said that they had complained often and loudly and nothing had been done. We arranged for the tables and chairs. The employees felt better about us and the project. They then became supportive of the new process, even though it meant additional work.

After you identify the problems, see which of these can be addressed fast and at low cost. We call these actions *quick hits*. Implementing some quick hits not only can improve the work and process, but also can generate more tolerance for the additional work later.

LACK OF AVAILABLE RESOURCES OR TIME TO SUPPORT THE CHANGE

DISCUSSION

Most business units and departments do not have extra people sitting around. So when the new project surfaces, the supervisors and managers are rightly fearful that if they assign their best people to the project, the productivity of the group will suffer. Often, they are right.

Yet many IT efforts insist that only senior users (the king and queen bees) be assigned to the project. This can cripple the user organization and poison employee feelings toward the change and the new process.

Impact

The basic direct impact of involving the best people is to deny their availability to their home departments. In one Latin American ERP installation the king and queen bees in three key departments were assigned 100% to the new system. Not only did the productivity of the departments suffer, but so did the financial results of the firm. Eventually, only parts of the ERP system were installed. The company could not bear any more pain.

Detection

You can detect whether there will be a resource problem by observing the user department. If the user work is specialized and spread across the employees, then when one is made available for the project, there will be a large gap back in the user department.

Actions and Prevention

Why do you need the senior users? Because they have the most knowledge. But what are you trying to do? Do you really want to automate 100 exceptions. Also, the new system will be used mostly by junior people.

We suggest that you involve junior users in the project at the start. You can get the senior people on a very limited basis if there is a crisis. This places fewer demands on the management of the departments. It will also bring into the project individuals who are more likely to be supportive of change.

TECHNOLOGY OR CHANGE THAT IS TOO COMPLICATED

Discussion

While some people are comfortable with change and new technology and others even embrace it, the majority have a hard time adapting and using the new technology. As an example, consider videotape recorders (VCRs). A survey showed that many blink the time 12:00:00. The people have no interest or desire even to set the clock on the equipment. It is the same with automobiles. Some people never change the time when daylight savings comes. It is just too much trouble.

Experience shows that very few people use many of the features of software that they have. For example, in word processing, how many features are you familiar with and do you use? A very small percentage.

IMPACT

The complexity of the new technology can frighten many people. When PCs were introduced in the 1980s, it was thought that most employees would embrace them right away. How wrong they were! Many companies had to establish end user computing groups and additional training. Even then some people just played solitaire or mine sweeper.

The complexity can turn people off. They get fearful, and the fear gets in the way of using the new system, technology, or process. Their productivity can be lower than it was with the old systems.

DETECTION

You know that a problem is coming if the IT group, the project manager, or the consultant emphasizes how the new system is revolutionary to the employees. They think they are generating excitement among the employees. In reality, they are generating something different — fear and dread.

ACTIONS AND PREVENTION

Play down the new technology and systems. Treat it like a black box. These are tools and means to the end — the new process. Play up the new process and how much easier it is. This is same approach that car salespeople use with potential customers. They first show them the standard features and functions so that the customer can become more comfortable. They might hint at some of the exotic features, but, unless the customer shows interest, this is a turnoff. In one case, the salesman violated this rule and showed a customer the rear camera and radar that could detect distance from the rear of the car. The customer became so involved with this, he did not realize that he was in forward gear. He accelerated and hit the car ahead.

POSSIBLE JOB LOSS

DISCUSSION

Job loss has been a common fear of change and automation for decades and longer. However, if you look at most system implementations, they either created jobs or, more often, changed the nature of the work. Clerical tasks were reduced so that employees could do other things — analytical work or customer service.

Another basic truth is that many companies are already thinned down and downsized. They are at the point where they do not want to lose good, experienced employees. In some countries, such as in Western Europe, it is difficult to terminate employees. Nevertheless, there is the fear that "my job will be lost when the new system goes in."

IMPACT

The impact of this fear can be resistance. Maybe the new system can be delayed and people can keep their jobs longer. Another fear is that of the unknown. They do not know what will happen to them and their work. So many people assume the worst possible outcome.

The fear can spread through a misstatement by a project leader when discussing benefits. Then the rumors begin to fly. Productivity drops.

DETECTION

Rather than detecting this fear, assume that it is there, but unstated.

ACTIONS AND PREVENTION

When you begin a project and collect information from users, this is where you have to start allaying the fear. Tell them what happens in similar installations: Most of the time people end up doing the same work or more of the interesting work.

After the requirements have been gathered, you should work with the user managers and Human Resources Department to go over the likely change in the nature of the work. You can help in preparing new job descriptions. Also, encourage the user managers and HR to develop a transition plan for staffing to the new system.

In one electric motor manufacturing facility in Asia, it was clear from the start that people would be made redundant. What did we do? Before starting the project, we identified work that needed to be done but was not being done. We found that testing, maintenance, training, and lessons learned were in short supply. We went over the list, first with employees and then with management. Then we proceeded to develop the requirements and identify the savings. In the meantime the HR manager started to map people into new jobs. When implementation time came for the new system, most of the people who were to be displaced had been moved into new positions.

RESISTING CHANGE BECAUSE WHAT HAS BEEN DONE IN THE PAST WORKED WELL

DISCUSSION

This is a basic factor behind resistance to change. If it works and has worked, it is not broken. Why fix it? In fact, you do this with many things around your house or apartment. Until some appliance breaks, you will not replace it. You are familiar with it and are not drawn to the new models with the additional features since your current one is still working.

IMPACT

If people are happy with what they have and how they do their work, then it will be very hard to convince them to change. The worst thing you can do is to wait until the rollout of the new system to discover this problem. You just do not have sufficient time to undo it and change their minds.

The impact may be that the people sit through the training. Then they go back to their work and behave as if the training never occurred. They will tend to keep resisting the new process since nothing has been done to change their attitudes.

DETECTION

You can detect this problem when you initially talk with employees about their work. If they do not bring up any problems, then you can assume they are relatively satisfied. Or they have been beaten down by the king and queen bees and now accept their fate.

Another approach is to go out where people smoke or where they take breaks. Sit down and pretend to read a magazine, book, or newspaper. Listen to what they talk about. Many people will discuss sports, family matters, etc. They will also share complaints and feelings about the work. In an interview they may be very positive about the work; in the breaks with their colleagues, they are very very different.

ACTIONS AND PREVENTION

The first step in systems analysis with the users is to identify problems in the current work. This must be accomplished with their involvement. After you have learned about some problems, you can bounce these off other employees. Then you can move onto the impacts of the problems. This will pave the way for the future change. Here is the basic truth:

**People have to admit they have problems before they
are willing to change.**

INABILITY TO TEACH AN OLD DOG NEW TRICKS

DISCUSSION

This issue applies to the king and queen bees. They have informal power. They have been there for a long time. They really like things the way they are. The same applies to some senior IT programmers.

If you think you can force these people to change, think again. Let's suppose that you get them to attend training in some new method or tool. After the training you oversee them for a while to observe whether they use the new method. Therein lies the problem. You cannot be there to watch them all of the time. They will revert back to their old ways.

IMPACT

If management tries to force them to change, you get the impact described earlier. Another approach is to leave them alone. However, this has problems and impacts as well. Their not being involved may be a sign to other employees that the new method or tool is going to fail.

DETECTION

When you are out in user departments, you will run into several king and queen bees. Here is what you can do to detect the degree of their resistance: Propose some minor changes and suggestions. See how they respond. If they dismiss them out of hand, then you know that they fit this issue.

ACTIONS AND PREVENTION

Well, forcing them to do things did not work. Leaving them totally alone fails. What is left? What do you do? Here is an approach that works: Concentrate your effort on the common transactions and work. Go to them and say,

"Look, we know you do exceptions and the odd work. There is just too much of that and too little time to address all of the exceptions." This will get their attention. Now propose that they continue to do what they do. The only thing you want is for them to provide information on the most frequent exceptions. You also want to encourage them to support the change.

This approach helps to neutralize the king and queen bees. It will not get them on your side if they still like the ways things have been. But at least they are less likely to cause problems or resist change. Moreover, after the changes have been implemented or during implementation you can revisit the exceptions and give them your undivided attention.

CHANGE THAT IS TOO RISKY

DISCUSSION

This is a real business fear. If you make a major change that affects many employees or customers, you could damage the business. Consider Sears. Many years ago they implemented bar coding. However, they did not implement scanning. This was a complete disaster. Clerks had to enter long codes exactly right. Lines grew very long. People walked out of the stores.

In response to risk, some people like to have backup or contingency plans. However, this can lead everyone to think that the backup plan was the real one. In the days of Spanish galleons and exploration, Spanish captains learned fast that they should send the ships away. In one case with a mutinous crew, the captain sank the ship. Why? Because then there is no way out or back. They had to go ahead — forward.

IMPACT

If people think that the change is too risky, it is difficult to dissuade them. Despite all of the talking, the risk and fear remain. This can demoralize any change effort.

DETECTION

When someone comes up with an idea for a new system or process, he or she typically gives the benefits but does not discuss risks. Pose the question "What can go wrong?" This should get some interesting comments. You can later posit more detailed scenarios.

ACTIONS AND PREVENTION

When Citibank rolled out the first ATM (automated teller machine), they spent a great deal of time looking into potential failures and disasters. This was a major effort and viewed as very risky, since no one had ever seen an ATM. It was successful and today we take this technology for granted.

The guideline here is to plan for the most likely things that can go wrong. If you plan for every potential problem, you will never implement anything.

NO ONE TAKING RESPONSIBILITY WHEN THE CHANGE DOES NOT WORK

DISCUSSION

This is always the case. Everyone wants to claim credit for success. No one wants to be the father of failure. The fear that some change will fail leads to the feeling that if one supports the change and it does not work, one will be blamed.

IMPACT

At the root of this issue is the concern that the change will not work and the associated people will get the blame. This leads people to try and avoid involvement in the new project.

DETECTION

Sometimes you can uncover this fear and concern by asking about what happened in the past with previous change efforts. If the organization found it necessary to label someone a scapegoat, then they have the fear and it is realistic.

ACTIONS AND PREVENTION

One approach is to try to ensure that the new system will work. Although this is obvious, it leads to some useful actions. We have already discussed finding quick hits when you are investigating the current process. These are things that will help the users and yield benefit with little cost or effort. Politi-

Vendors, Consultants, and Outsourcing

INTRODUCTION

Problems with outsourcing go back thousands of years. Records from ancient Egypt document issues in managing mercenary troops. Ancient Roman and Greek records detail methods and problems in managing servants. Machiavelli, in the book *The Prince*, gave instructions on managing mercenary troops. Many of these ideas remain valid today.

Outsourcing has increased as firms try to implement new systems and technology. Firms outsource support activities, such as maintenance, network operations, help desk, and other work. Why do outsourcing issues arise and surprise people? Because even with a great deal of planning, you find that all outsourcing requires constant management and coordination. Some people assume that if you get the vendor started on the work, it will go all right. This is not a good assumption.

INADEQUATE VENDOR PERFORMANCE

DISCUSSION

A common complaint in surveys of outsourcing is that the vendor's performance either is highly variable or deteriorates over time. In any case, the work is inadequate. That could mean problems with the quality of the work, the timeliness of work, or what the vendor is really doing.

When you assign people to do the work, you cannot assume that they will do as you say. Everyone puts his or her own spin and stamp on it, with interpretation based on past experience, methods, and tools. If you assign work to a contractor project leader along with expectations of quality, there is no guarantee that this will be translated correctly to the vendor technical staff.

IMPACT

In addition to higher cost and longer schedules for the work to be performed right, there is the political cost in the relationship between the customer and the supplier. The firm and the individuals who interface with the vendor begin to lose faith in the vendor's ability to deliver.

As this deterioration occurs, the customer may try to find another vendor. The customer may consider having internal staff do the work. All of this requires more effort.

DETECTION

You should have quality reviews. Never accept it as truth when the vendor says everything is fine and on schedule. In one case, the vendor assured an insurance company that they would get a new version of the software. Then they said it would be delayed, but gave a certain delivery date. The date came and went and nothing materialized. Finally, the vendor told the firm that they were going out of business. There would be no support and certainly no new version.

How was this allowed to happen? No one in the insurance company was assigned to coordinate with the vendor. The only contact occurred when there was a problem or question. The insurance firm assumed the vendor was stable. They did not notice until it was too late that each time they called, they were handled by a different person. No one put things together to get the whole picture.

ACTIONS AND PREVENTION

Start with the fact that any vendor acts in their own self-interest. This is obvious and true for all of the issues in this chapter. You want to achieve a reasonable level of knowledge and control about the vendor's activities.

When work begins, carefully review the initial work. This will set a pattern of behavior. The vendor will learn what level of quality you want. Don't stop there. Keep at it. Have one person assigned to oversee the vendor work. More guidelines will be given later in the chapter.

On an ongoing basis, track how the vendor performs when resolving problems and issues. This can be an early warning sign of quality problems. It is definitely preferred to resolve this early than to let it escalate to the Service Level Agreement (SLA) or the contract.

VENDOR STAFF WHO DO NOT SHARE INFORMATION

DISCUSSION

Individual vendor staff may not want to share their methods and tools because of fear that they could be copied or misused. They may even fear sharing these with other employees at the same vendor. If this is the case, they sure will not want to share them with the IT staff.

Another reason this issue arises stems from customer behavior. Many firms show no interest in how the work is performed. They just want results. This message reaches the vendor loud and clear when they attempt to tell the IT staff how they are doing the work. The internal staff have more than enough other work to do and see no reason to learn about what the vendor is doing. This problem then can lead to quality problems later.

IMPACT

You might think that providing documentation constitutes sufficient sharing of knowledge. However, you can see from automobiles that the manual you got with the vehicle is insufficient. You learn much more about the car when you talk to mechanics who have to repair or maintain the same type of car.

If the information is not shared, then when problems or questions arise, you have to call the vendor often and very early in the problem-solving process. They may help you initially but then become more resistant as you continue to make calls. The customer staff then start to feel helpless. Every time something happens, they have to stop and call the vendor. Productivity and the value of the vendor services decline.

DETECTION

Early in the vendor's work you can ask about how they do the work. You can probe into what methods and tools they use or will use. This can be performed as part of vendor evaluation.

During the vendor work you can visit the vendor premises and talk to the group that is doing work for you. Show interest in how they do their work. If they resist or do not volunteer information, you know you have a problem.

ACTIONS AND PREVENTION

At the start of the work and even in contract negotiation, you can spell out what and how information is to be transferred from the vendor to your organization. You can test this agreement early in the work. Raise information transfer or the lack of it as an issue at early stages of the work.

You can employ the suggestions in the previous section for prevention. You should also inform the vendor that you expect and require sharing of information. Here are some additional actions you can take.

• Have a common list of issues. For each issue assigned to the vendor, find out how they went about solving the issue.

• When they complete some work, have them present it to the internal staff. Encourage the internal employees to ask questions.

• Implement a policy of shared tasks between the vendor and internal employees. While it is impractical and unrealistic to do this on a broad scale, you can do it on a limited basis.

• Focus the information sharing on areas of risk that have issues. This will reduce the scope of the effort in sharing information.

• Organize the information provided by the vendor. Otherwise, it will probably be forgotten.

VENDORS THAT USE THEIR OWN PROPRIETARY METHODS AND TOOLS

DISCUSSION

Everyone has tips and tricks. Software vendors have their own routines and utilities that have been developed and honed over many projects. Most vendors view these as proprietary and part of their competitive advantage.

IMPACT

If you always are going to use this particular vendor, then the issue may be significant. However, if you think the work may be shifted to another vendor or moved in-house, then this is an issue.

VENDOR THAT WAS POLITICALLY SELECTED BY MANAGEMENT

DISCUSSION

In a small organization, the head of the firm often selects vendors based on who they know and on their past experiences with them. In a large organization, you might think this could not happen. However, it still does. The CEO or president may have personal or even family ties with another firm. There could also be ties through management associations, country clubs, etc.

IMPACT

The impact is similar to that when the head of the firm brings in a young relative to work in an organization. The person has to be treated differently by everyone. All know that the person is "favored." Having a politically selected individual or firm creates many issues. If the individual or firm is assigned work and fails, there are problems. If you go to the boss and say the firm is incompetent or cannot do the work well, *you* will likely be viewed as the problem. Remember: In the movies it is the bearer of bad tidings who is executed.

Work is affected. The relationship between employees and the outside firm is tenuous at best. Issues are not addressed because they are too politically sensitive.

Alternatively, the vendor may see the work as the result of the ties. As such, they may not assign their best people to the work; it is just part of the relationship.

DETECTION

Try to find out how the vendor got the work. Here are some other questions to answer.

- How did they learn about the work?
- Who do they know in the company?
- Did they do work with the organization before?
- With whom did they do their previous work?

This will help uncover links you might not have discovered otherwise.

ACTIONS AND PREVENTION

Forget prevention — turn to actions. If you find out that someone is going to be given or is given the work, narrow the scope of that work. Ahead of time, you might divide up the project and isolate some of the nonrisky work to be awarded to the firm favored by the manager.

If the firm is selected, you should conduct a frank meeting with the vendor. Indicate that you are aware of the ties with management. Tell them that you have no problem with that as long as they do the work. Also, indicate that you might want to use them to get some messages directly through to upper management. In the past this is how we have turned this issue into an opportunity.

VENDOR THAT DOES NOT RESOLVE ISSUES

Discussion

You have identified an issue that falls under the vendor's scope and work. The vendor is assigned the issue. The issue never seems to be completely resolved. Promises are made and not kept.

Why doesn't the vendor want to solve the issue? It often is a difficult and political one for the vendor manager. Any solution would create problems for the vendor manager. So the issue gets put off.

Impact

As you observed in the first part of the book, the longer a major issue goes unresolved, the greater the impact. The issue can grow so that it has to be addressed at higher organizational levels.

Then there is the direct impact on the work. In addition to delay, wasted work may be done. The relationship between the customer and the vendor suffers.

Detection

You want to use the issues tracking in Chapter 2 here. Make sure that the vendor and you have the same list of issues. In this manner you can track how fast and how completely the vendor solves the problems. You can also determine whether solving one issue generated new ones.

Actions and Prevention

Issues management is a main way to prevent the problem. In vendor evaluation, make issues management a key part of the evaluation. Have potential vendors explain how they define priorities in dealing with issues.

Another step is to focus on issues in regular meetings. Here is another tip. Separate meetings on status from meetings on issues. In a status meeting you can identify an issue and determine where it stands. This leaves little time for addressing the issue in depth. That is why you want separate meetings on issues. They receive undivided attention from the vendor and you.

When the issue has been identified, do not assume that the vendor understands. You should have the vendor feed the issue back to you. In addition, make sure that the vendor understands the importance of the issue and the impact if it is not resolved.

VENDOR TEAM LEADER WHO MISCOMMUNICATES TO VENDOR STAFF

DISCUSSION

This is the common problem of secondhand information. In our experience, this issue has led directly to the failure of many projects and IT work. When you hire a vendor, the vendor has to identify a project leader. This is the person through whom you will channel your communications. Therein lies the problem.

In one government agency, the project leader was trained as a user. He was given a lot of information about the business processes and the systems. He nodded his head each time and told the customer that he would relay all of this to the programmers on the vendor side.

The first sign of failure occurred when the prototype of the system was shown. It did not fit the business situation at all. The customer had assumed that the project leader would accurately and completely relay the information. This did not happen. The vendor management went into panic mode and replaced the project leader. The work started all over again. The problem was never solved. Failure resulted.

IMPACT

The impact of the issue is that the vendor staff may be given the wrong information or, at best, incomplete information. This is normally unknown to the customer, who thinks everything is OK. The problem is only discovered later.

The schedule suffers. Much of the previous work was wasted. Work must be redone. There are bad feelings all around.

DETECTION

When you relate information to the vendor liaison, have that individual feed it back to you in writing. Then have a meeting with the vendor employees. This is one way to detect the problem. You do not want to wait as long as the government agency in our example.

ACTIONS AND PREVENTION

To prevent this problem, train the vendor employees who will do the work in your terminology and process. Insist on this — even if it incrementally raises the cost. Another action is to hold regular meetings with not only the vendor project leader, but also the technical people.

Do the same with issues for which the vendor is responsible. Get down to the people who will act on the issue. You cannot do this for every issue. However, you can concentrate on the major ones with higher risk.

Another step can be taken at the start of the work. Then you can carefully define the vendor project leader role and point to this issue. This will make the vendor aware of the problem.

VENDOR THAT OVERPROMISES

DISCUSSION

Salespeople of the vendors will often make many claims and even promises. They may see that as part of what is required to get the work. Most people know this. That is why vendor claims and promises are checked out in detail during the vendor selection process.

There is less attention after the award of the work. People tend to trust the vendor project leader. After all, he or she is not a salesperson. Right? This is not a good idea. Follow the old axiom "Trust but verify." The approach laid out for this issue focuses on the communications with the vendor.

IMPACT

A promise not kept is a promise broken. The vendor loses credibility with the customer. The internal IT staff members begin to make jokes about the vendor promises. The vendor–customer relationship suffers.

Headquarters

INTRODUCTION

The problem of relations between headquarters and division has occurred for thousands of years. Many of the problems in this chapter occurred and have been documented in ancient China, Rome, and Egypt. This can lead you logically to believe that while there is much new in the world over time, many issues recur repeatedly in diverse situations.

In this chapter we refer to headquarters. But this could be the main office of a medium-size organization such as a local government or firm. It can also refer to firms that have international operations. A large university, such as the University of California, has some or all of these issues: many political entities, individual academic departments, central administration in a particular location, systemwide administration (headquarters), and administrative support groups. It does not stop there, for there are also the governor and the legislature.

HEADQUARTERS DICTATING A SOLUTION

DISCUSSION

Managers at headquarters want standardized information. In addition, they want standardized systems. The underlying thinking sometimes is that the divisions or business units are involved in tactical work, so it is headquarters' role to determine and set strategic direction.

Nowhere is this more apparent than in IT. Often, the impetus for an ERP system comes from headquarters. They have the money. The vendors know that approval of such a large expenditure and project must come from headquarters. So they concentrate their marketing on the IT group and management at headquarters. Headquarters IT–related staff are often tasked with architecture and technology assessment. Division-level IT staff members are tied up in daily production, support, and local projects.

Impact

If the solution has been thoroughly thought through and if headquarters has worked closely with a range — most or all of the business units — this can work. It can work well. Then all may benefit.

However, experience shows that this is somewhat infrequent. These are major "ifs." Here are some of the problems.

- No one really thought through the impact of implementation at the business unit level.
- No one considered how to handle production and coordination.
- The cost of implementation may have been dramatically underestimated.
- There may be little benefit of the solution to the business units.
- The vendor may not provide support in certain countries.

Wait a minute. The issue involves the word *solution*. Doesn't this mean a solution for all? Not necessarily. It is a solution in the eyes of the beholder — in this case, headquarters. Some ERP implementations, while providing data to headquarters and, consequently, benefits, result in more work and data capture at the business unit. For them, in this instance, there may be little or no benefit, only more effort with the same resources and same demands for sales, production, etc.

Detection

This problem can be detected by examining how headquarters units involve the business unit IT staff and business managers in IT-related planning and technology. Little communication is a good sign of problems to come.

Actions and Prevention

The best approach is to develop an overall IT architecture that includes both local and headquarters systems and technology. Local needs, as well as headquarters requirements, have to be met in this architecture.

If this cannot be done, then in the planning for the selected solution, the business units can be included. A good method is to determine what problems in other areas exist at the business unit level. These can be included in the scope of the overall solution. Thus, while the business unit employees have to do more work in production, they also got some of their problems solved. This is our major approach in implementing major integrated systems such as ERP systems.

NO ALLOWANCE FOR RESOURCE NEEDS AT THE LOCAL LEVEL

DISCUSSION

At the local level, the IT staff is often consumed in support, maintenance, and operations. What little time is left over is spent on responding to local management and user requirements that cannot be handled by the overall systems.

Headquarters units sometimes do not take this into account. They may feel that the effort to implement a new technology or system is not that demanding. Unless they have done it before this, this could be a problem.

Another perception is that if consultants are hired to work at the local level, they can make up for any resource shortfall. However, the consultants still require time and effort of the local people.

IMPACT

If the solution is put on the table and the resource needs are not considered, then system implementation becomes more work for the local people — on top of what they already have to do. They may react with many problems and complaints. A common question is "Do you want us to make money and do our work? Or should we give priority to the new system?" If local management can intimidate headquarters management on a business level, then the project may be quietly shelved.

Even worse, what was planned for universal deployment may become localized. Some divisions do it all. Some do none. Others do parts of the implementation. Benefits are then reduced.

DETECTION

As with most of the issues in this chapter, the problem can be detected by reviewing the communication between headquarters and divisions. To what extent is the resource issue raised? More important, is this issue raised by headquarters? If it is, this indicates some sensitivity and recognition that there is a resource issue.

ACTIONS AND PREVENTION

Resource planning should be carried out early. One key step is to have each business unit try to free up resources by reducing any new work. They might say that support cannot be reduced. Left on their own, support and maintenance can consume all available time and people. So can some of the maintenance work be deferred? The key question to address is "What if the work is not performed or is delayed?"

Overall, a life cycle plan is needed where the costs and support are pinned down not only for implementation but also for operations. The new system should be viewed from different perspectives — headquarters, local units, customers.

HEADQUARTERS ATTEMPTING TO MICROMANAGE THE WORK IN THE BUSINESS UNIT

DISCUSSION

This is relatively rare, for business reasons. The business units are normally accountable for revenue and costs, so they are left alone and monitored. However, it can happen if the system or new technology is major in scope and scale. Then the business unit might not have the expertise. It would take too long to create the experience and knowledge locally, so headquarters thinks it should be closely managed.

IMPACT

American leaders during the Vietnam War attempted to micromanage from thousands of miles away with interpreted, delayed intelligence. Needless to say, it did not work well. Today, commanders in the field have more discretion. They should have learned from Stalin. When he tried to micromanage the war with Nazi Germany, he failed. When he delegated, he won.

DETECTION

You can detect this problem if headquarters starts to provide detailed guidelines. You can also see the problem coming if the headquarters staff are spend-

IMPACT

The impact of miscommunication can mean extra, unneeded work at both the headquarters and business unit levels. Wait — it can get worse. The miscommunication can lead to mistrust. Information must be verified. Decisions and actions are delayed, impacting the business.

DETECTION

First, start to detect the problem by observing the number of communications between the business units and headquarters. More is generally better. Second, see if many of the communications are formal. Informal communications are better here and tend to head off communication problems. Third, observe if there are e-mails asking for clarification and questions raised about what seems relatively obvious.

ACTIONS AND PREVENTION

One approach that some firms and organizations employ is to rotate managers back and forth between headquarters and business units as well as between business units. This can reduce the number of communication problems.

Another approach is to encourage informal communications and to structure the formal communications more completely. We have taken the step to have someone play the role of the business unit. In this position the person attempts to give a range of interpretations to the communications. These steps can head off many difficult problems later.

TOO FREQUENT TURNOVER AND CHANGE OF HEADQUARTERS PEOPLE

DISCUSSION

To many in the business units, headquarters seems remote. They get e-mails and memos that some new manager was named. Most of the time the business units take it in stride and just go back to business. The change does not affect them — yet.

Some turnover at headquarters is natural. It is sometimes more frequent because of the nature of the work. At the headquarters level, unless you are in a support role, you are not hands-on. Many managers like to be hands-on. But they can only bear a certain amount of time at this. They get frustrated and leave. You see this in managers who are named to very high positions and then leave soon after.

IMPACT

There is little or no impact if the new managers do not make changes. However, many new managers want to put their mark or stamp on the organization. If you make changes at headquarters, the changes are not big. Many headquarters staffs are small. The scope of work and decisions is limited. So what better way to make an imprint than to dictate change to one or more business units.

We saw this at a petroleum firm in Asia. The outfit was owned by two foreign partners. One had a very structured approach to management; the other did the opposite. There was a minimum of structure. In itself this would not have been an issue. However, the management approach to running the Asian firm was to rotate managers every year. Odd-numbered years saw a manager from one firm there. In even-numbered years a manager from the other firm was assigned. This created havoc with the IT staff. They would no sooner start big projects than the managers were rotated. No major work was completed.

DETECTION

You would determine if there was a problem by viewing and witnessing it at the business unit level. It was this way in the example just cited. Productivity and morale were low. The staff felt absolutely helpless. There was then more turnover of IT staff locally.

ACTIONS AND PREVENTION

We can identify acts to prevent and deal with the issue through the example. The company policy in the example could not be changed; it was part of the charter of the Asian firm. What could be done? A two-tiered steering committee was initiated. The upper tier was led by the manager from the parent firm; the lower tier dealt with most issues.

A second step was to link all projects and work to key business processes. The rotating managers were not, as a result, inclined to disrupt the work. The people doing the work were more motivated because they saw results and completed work.

The third step was to overlap the two managers for one month. Even longer would have been better, but this was impossible. The overlap gave a chance for

ACTIONS AND PREVENTION

Headquarters IT should consider the impact of the directive. The planning approach and motivation discussed earlier can be applied here.

Imposing many decisions on divisions often requires money, unless it is a general policy or procedure. Even additional reporting costs money to implement. What should the business unit do? If funding is nonexistent, then seek to implement it in a minimal level through interpretation. You would also, of course, raise the issue of money with headquarters.

ISSUES AND QUESTIONS RAISED WITH HEADQUARTERS THAT ARE NOT BEING ADDRESSED

DISCUSSION

We and you have probably seen this happen many times. Business unit IT raises questions with their counterparts at headquarters. Headquarters IT says they will look into it. Nothing happens. Why not? One reason is that only one business unit raised the issue. If no one else raised the problem, then it must not be a problem. Right? That is how some at headquarters think.

Another reason that an issue or question is not answered is that headquarters IT may be politically weak and not have sufficient power or authority to deal with it. However, they do not want to reveal weakness. You know that few individuals do, so this is consistent.

IMPACT

What does the business unit IT group do? They try several times and nothing happens. They could escalate the issue through the business managers. This is perilous because the IT group in the business unit shows that it is too weak to get a decision. Moreover, you do not know what will happen if business managers who do not know IT suddenly have to get involved in IT matters. It is a "crap shoot." Maybe it will be OK, but probably not.

A more likely scenario is that the business unit IT group will make assumptions and take what they consider to be reasonable actions. Later, this could be a problem. Why? Because a decision or answer may come down that is opposite or in conflict with their direction.

Detection

What unresolved questions and issues does each division have with head-quarters IT? How long have these things been sitting there awaiting an answer? What is the impact of lack of response on the business? These are some of the questions to answer to ascertain the severity of the problem.

Actions and Prevention

One action to be imposed by IT management is that both sides — headquarters and the business units — should track the open issues, each one by date, requester, severity, and type. Part of the review of IT should be on the resolution of issues and responsiveness.

Another step is to apply more structure to questions and requests. Here are some reasonable areas to cover:

- What is the problem?
- How did the problem arise?
- What is the impact if the problem on the business unit is not addressed?
- What is the time urgency of the problem?

The second question is that of value, because many times a business unit may misinterpret something. This is why only one business unit is asking a question that applies to others.

CONCLUSIONS

The relationship between headquarters IT and that of the business units is often addressed in an ad hoc, incident-by-incident manner. This leads to problems. Sometimes the IT managers on both sides rely on their personal working relationships. This can also be a problem when there is a management change. It is better to have consistent structure.

Chapter 12

Technology

INTRODUCTION

This chapter considers technology in general, with some limited emphasis on software. The life cycle and software packages are addressed in Part IV of the book. Technology issues involve assessment, evaluation, implementation, operation, obsolescence, and replacement. Of course, you can take the approach of not adopting new technology. Some people do this. We did this with an old car. It was 20 years old and running fine. What happened? Why did we have to get rid of it? It became difficult to maintain. Parts were no longer available from the automobile dealer. We had to go to a junkyard and take parts off of a wrecked car. Each minor replacement was a big project that took all day as we drove around to find a suitable car and then remove the part. Difficulty in maintenance is one cause. Another is that the technology becomes obsolete and lacks new functions. That happened too. The car did not pass the smog emission rules and so would have to have been junked anyhow.

A general problem is that firms and individuals do not consider the technology carefully. They treat each new technology as separate. People think that since each experience is unique, lessons are to be learned. This is as far from the truth as you can get. You could probably adapt a checklist for buying a new camera or car to evaluating hardware.

MERGING AND COMBINING OF TECHNOLOGY VENDORS

DISCUSSION

This occurs in hardware, software, and networking. In the hardware and networking arenas the reason is often to acquire the technology and then remarket it. They can then expand and retain the market.

In software the situation is more complex. Some firms, like Computer Associates, grow by acquisition. Others, like Microsoft, buy a firm to acquire software capabilities and the supporting technical staff. It is faster, cheaper, and easier than doing all of the development in-house. Moreover, they are buying a proven product.

The third path is for one software firm to acquire another software firm. Then the firm is getting an expanded customer base and market share. This is the Oracle and PeopleSoft approach. J.D. Edwards was acquired by PeopleSoft, which in turn was acquired by Oracle — small fish being consumed by a larger fish, consumed by an even larger fish.

IMPACT

There is limited risk in the hardware and network areas due to standardization and compatibility. The major issue lies in application software. The danger is twofold. First, the new vendor will not likely want to issue new versions of the acquired software. They want you to convert to theirs. If the acquired firm's software was super successful, then the acquiree would become the acquirer.

The second danger is more serious. While the first one is a problem in the intermediate term, there is the peril that the new vendor will not support the acquired company's software. Some of the people that supported the older software may see the writing on the wall and bail out.

DETECTION

Keep looking in the Internet magazines for news about the firm that provided your software. Also, go to the company Website and examine their financial statements and reports. Then search for evaluations of software packages in the same category.

ACTIONS AND PREVENTION

You can almost predict whether your vendor will be acquired based on some or all of the following factors:

- Sales trends
- Issuance of new products
- Availability of upgrades and new versions
- Quality of support for the software
- Strengthening position of the competition

Also, keep up to date on what other, similar vendors are offering.

cials. All cars do the same thing. They get you from A to B. So what do they emphasize? Looks, style, features that are marginal.

Review the literature and try to discern what the benefits really are. Do these apply to your organization? Keep in mind that many articles in trade magazines are either written by or strongly influenced by the vendor. This is actually good, since the benefits will be stated in optimistic terms. If this rosy view of the product is not particularly good, then you might want to pass on the technology.

ACTIONS AND PREVENTION

Use this issue to assist you in evaluating technology. Insist on tangible benefits. Consider the life cycle costs of the technology. Then to balance this, you can consider the option of not using the technology and keeping things as they are.

NEED FOR A DECISION AS TO WHETHER TO ADOPT A NEW TECHNOLOGY

DISCUSSION

This happens in your personal life quite often. Something new comes out and you wonder if you want to buy it and use it. Let's look at two examples — one of failure and one of success. We bought an early digital camera. This promised to free us up from photo processing. Costs would be lower. We could do our own photo printing. Wow! This looked good. Then as we used the camera, we found problems. First, the resolution was not very good. Second, the camera ate batteries like Godzilla eats cities. Third, the camera's operation was clumsy. Fourth, the camera did not store many photos. The impacts included: (1) it cost much more than anticipated; (2) it was more difficult to deal with than a 35 mm camera; (3) the lack of storage mandated either extra storage media or taking the computer on each trip. This was just the hardware side. On the software side, the available software to manipulate and improve the photos was pretty hard to work with. This was a disaster overall, and we threw the camera in the closet. From experience we have found that you want to hide technology that does not work. You can laugh at this example now. Things have significantly improved. The cameras, memory, batteries, and software are better. The technology works.

Now what did we learn from this? Do not buy too soon. Evaluate the entire end-to-end use of the technology. Consider support and maintenance, good things to apply to the business assessment of technology. Now let's see what we learned. Another technology was a camcorder. This replaced old, cumbersome VCR equipment, which in turn replaced the old 8 mm or 16 mm motion picture cameras. At first they looked attractive. But below the surface lurked issues: interface problems, variety of storage approaches, limited color and resolution. Decision? Wait. Then wait some more. Then the technology improved, with better storage and the three-chip color-processing technology. Time to buy. It is not likely to improve further in the short term.

IMPACT

There are two types of errors in statistics. The type 1 error is the more severe. In medical treatment this means that you would die from the medication. The type 2 error is less severe. The medicine would not make you sick; on the other hand, it would not make you well.

The type 1 error is that the business is impacted negatively because of your decision. The type 2 error is that the technology did not deliver the benefit but did not make it worse. Then, like the digital camera, it is thrown figuratively in the closet.

If you do not acquire the technology, then you missed the opportunities and benefits of the technology. On the other hand, you did not endure the pain and suffering of learning, installing, and working with the technology.

When you acquire the technology, you get the gain of the new functions and features. However, you have to change the business processes that relate to the new technology. You also have the effort and time associated with installation, setup, and operations.

What is the cost of a new technology? Here is a list of cost elements.

- Investigation of the technology
- Evaluation and determination of fit
- Installation of the technology
- Adaptation of the technology to your environment
- Learning the new technology
- Gaining expertise in the technology
- Application of the new technology
- Interfacing the new technology with the existing technology
- Removing some old technology and replacing it with the new
- Coercing people to use the new technology
- Measuring and justifying the new technology
- Support for the new technology

We purposely made this list long. Why? Politically, to dampen the enthusiasm and make people think more practically. Technically, to make people think about the effort. Remember that installing a new technology means a number of adjustments, including:

- Stopping the use of the old technology
- Migrating applications and dependent technologies to the new technology
- Establishing and stabilizing the new technology in production and operations

DETECTION

From experience we have found that a key factor is awareness. Some people get drawn toward the technology so that they tend to adopt it gradually. This is dangerous, since there is no systematic effort to analyze the benefits and risks associated with the technology.

Another sign of problems to come occurs when management adopts the technology without involving the IT staff in the evaluation. Management may then assume that IT can just make it work. They probably can, but at a high price in effort. An example of this occurred when a manager acquired a Blackberry PDA-phone device. The IT group was not familiar with it and then had to devote considerable resources to implementing the technology.

ACTIONS AND PREVENTION

In deciding whether to adopt a new technology, it's best to err on the side of caution. Go to the basic question.

What will happen if we do not adopt the technology?

This is the downside risk.

On the benefit-and-cost analysis, consider the life cycle costs, the range of application of the new technology, the likelihood of other, cheaper and similar products later.

There is a political danger for IT. If IT seems to be supporting the acquisition of the new technology, it may appear self-serving. Management may think that IT jumps at every new technology. It is much better to be neutral or negative. After all, what does IT get out of most new technology? More work and support — for the same pay.

INCOMPATIBILITY OF THE TECHNOLOGIES IN USE AND OF POTENTIAL USE

DISCUSSION

Compatibility is a major issue, in some cases the dominant problem. Compatibility problems exist in hardware, networking, software, and data. Of these, hardware and networking are the lesser ones most often.

For software and data there are often major differences between information of the old and new systems. Here are some of the differences.

• *Meaning of the data elements themselves.* The same named data element may have entirely diverse meanings and uses in the two systems.

• *Timing.* When data elements are updated is a potential issue.

• *Accuracy and level of detail.* The new system will often have much more detail. For example, older business systems did not support an extended 9-digit mail code in the U.S.A.

• *New information.* The new system contains additional data elements.

IMPACT

To many users, the differences just listed may appear minor. They get irritated when data conversion arises. Users have worked with the information in the old system for a long time. They see no problem. However, they may be using some fields for purposes that were not intended or planned during the implementation of the old system.

Another problem is shadow systems. The users may have additional analysis and business rules along with derived data elements here. These are, let's suppose, to be replaced by those in the new system. So there is some potentially unplanned or underestimated work in mapping the data elements and in understanding how the shadow systems work. Compounding this problem are two factors. First, the shadow systems may have no documentation. Second, the person who created the shadow systems is long gone.

Data conversion is a frequent problem, in our experience. There are significant issues here. The problem may not appear until the new system goes live. In one example, users told IT that the telephone number for the customer in the old system was valid. This was not verified. Then after training and conversion of the old data, the new system was put into production. Failure occurred because of that one data element. The entire project stopped while telephone numbers were converted from an unknown shadow system (that is, unknown to IT).

Chapter 13

IT Strategic Planning

INTRODUCTION

A number of different methods have been proposed for doing IT strategic planning. Many of these failed because they were not pragmatic. They were filled with jargon. They were not common sense. While the methods change, the issues associated with IT strategic planning often do not.

These issues can be divided into the following categories.

- The role of management and others in the planning process is not well defined.
- What people are supposed to do with the plan is not considered. The emphasis is on accomplishing the plan.
- What the plan is really intended to accomplish is not considered.
- How the plan elements are to be linked to the business is not clearly determined. This raises issues in alignment and impact of the plan on the business.
- Some people lose sight of the fact that the plan is just the plan. It does not, in and of itself, result in change.

Here are some general guidelines for IT strategic planning.

- Make sure you have some defined method for getting resources and money for the action items in the plan after the plan is approved.
- Involve as many managers and staff as you can, to get more support for the plan.
- Try to have about half of the action items in the plan be nonproject based. That is, they address policies, procedures, organization, roles, etc. — things that can be done without money.

- Develop the plans as lists and tables of issues, objectives, strategies, and action items that can be viewed easily and incrementally.

The discussion in this chapter relies on the following definitions.

- *Issues and opportunities.* These are both problems and potential good things that can be done related to IT.
- *Objectives.* These are directional goals for IT. They are timeless. If the objectives were achieved, the issues and opportunities would disappear.
- *Constraints.* These are conditions that you have to accept. Included here are the business focus, available money and staff, and existing technology. Constraints prevent the objectives from being quickly attained.
- *Strategies.* Strategies can be attained over a year or two. They are also general. Their purpose is get around the constraints, to get at the issues while supporting the objectives.
- *Action items.* These are specific things you can do to support the strategies and objectives. Contrary to what some think, action items do not mean just project ideas or candidates. They include policy, organization, roles, procedures, and other changes. In our experience, good plans have half or more of the action items in these nonproject categories.

LACK OF MANAGEMENT INTEREST ONCE THE PLAN IS APPROVED

Discussion

Effort and time were consumed in the IT plan creation. Management reviewed and approved the plan. Why on earth would they lose interest? Here are some possible reasons.

- The managers think that if they approve it, the plan will be executed.
- They think their role is over.
- Some managers do not want to get involved in implementation.

Whatever the reason, the work on potential projects identified in the action items of the plan has not started. The projects have not been funded. No resources have been allocated to the work. The resource issue is the major hurdle. You can make some money available, but there is a finite limit to the pool of qualified resources. It is a zero-sum game. If you give resources to some of the planning action items, you take them away from other work.

Impact

If management support ebbs, problems could arise in implementing the plan. People lose interest because they sense a bailout by management. The impact is that the plan ends up on the shelf — unused and ignored.

The negative effects now propagate. Without an effective IT plan, new technology can enter the organization on an ad hoc basis. There is less chance that the new project ideas in the plan will ever start and see the light of day. You might be able to salvage and implement some of the nonproject action items that require no money.

DETECTION

During the planning effort, is there any interest on management's part in what happens after the planning effort? Note that you are not looking for great interest. Upper management has many other activities and issues to deal with.

Maybe management will be interested in giving the money. But that is not enough. The key issue is what will be stopped, shelved, or delayed so that the resources can be placed on the project-oriented action items of the plan.

ACTIONS AND PREVENTION

One action that can be taken is to plan ahead for the resource issues. During the planning effort, you might review the progress of the current projects and nonproject work. There is a political reason for the strategic IT plan. IT management may want to control support and maintenance work as well as to shelve some smaller projects or projects that are not doing well. One benefit and purpose of the IT plan is to provide a basis for making these rather difficult political decisions.

During the planning effort, you want to alert managers that resource issues will arise later. This is a valuable early warning. You cannot assume that upper management is aware of the resource constraints in IT. They may perceive that IT managers complain a lot but still get the work done. So what if you pile on a few more projects?

DIFFICULTY LINKING IT PLANNING FACTORS TO THE BUSINESS

DISCUSSION

Business objectives, mission, and vision are vague and fuzzy. IT objectives are more precise. Let's give an example. Suppose an element of the mission statement is "To improve the efficiency and effectiveness of work and operations." Now turn to an IT action item: "Implement a new network monitoring system." Very precise and specific. How do you link these? It appears to be very difficult. Actually, it is not.

Let's move up from the action item to an IT strategy. An applicable IT strategy is "Improve network performance, reliability, and availability." OK, that fits as an umbrella over the action item, but you are a long way from the mission element.

Now move up to the IT objective. One that would fit here is "Implement improved and modernized IT infrastructure." This fits too, since the network is part of the infrastructure. But you are still not linked to the mission element.

What does an "improved and modernized IT infrastructure" have to do with the business? How does it help the business? Well, the core business processes rely on automation and systems. This means that the performance of the business processes depends on stable and high-performance infrastructure.

What has been covered so far? You went from a detailed action item to the IT strategy and then to the IT objective. Then you linked the IT objective to the business processes. But you are not there yet. What next? You must come down from the lofty heights of the mission to the business processes. The improvement of work and operations translates into effective business processes.

The underlying message is that the linkage of IT planning to the mission, vision, or objectives is easiest and most supported through business processes. This inherently makes sense because a basic goal of IT is to support processes. Another purpose is to provide management with information. Coming from the business side, there is no way you can attain any business goal without high business process performance.

IMPACT

Because of this perceived difficulty, people often stop in the IT planning effort with the IT objectives. Then there is no linkage to the business factors. Management and business units can then question the value of the plan. They may raise the issue of whether IT is aligned to the business. In the most negative terms, they may question the investment in IT.

DETECTION

If the IT planning effort concentrates on the IT factors, then you can sense a problem. The analysis of the business side has to be performed during the planning effort. In fact, this is a good place to start. Map the mission, vision, or objectives to the business processes.

ACTIONS AND PREVENTION

To prevent the problem, follow the guidance in the preceding paragraph. If you find that the planning effort is becoming overfocused on the IT factors, then you can take corrective action to work on the business factors.

HIGH MANAGEMENT EXPECTATIONS OF THE PLANNING EFFORT

DISCUSSION

Management typically likes an IT plan. They know the importance of IT. They may not know much about the systems and technology. It may appear as a foreign language. Today, however, few managers do not realize the need for IT.

Earlier we discussed what happens if there is no effective plan. Without repeating that discussion, remember that the IT plan can be seen by management as a way of understanding all of the different IT activities from a managerial perspective.

Given that managers see the value of the plan, what would senior managers expect? First, they may have little experience in this. Second, they may want IT to work on more strategic projects and work. They may see IT as doing tactical stuff. They may feel they are not getting their money's worth. So the reasonable expectation is that if they approve the plan, IT will shift to a more strategic focus.

IMPACT

High expectations are one thing; reality is another. You can have a wonderful, approved plan. However, you could be locked into some existing projects. Maintenance and support consume a high percentage of resources. Management may want IT to perform wonders but still not provide the money and resources as well as support for process change and improvement.

What is the effect of all of this? The expectations of management are not met. Management is disappointed. They think they have given IT enough. They see the plan as work substitution in IT. Well, it cannot be the fault of management. So who allocates the resources in IT? The IT manager. Blame him or her for the problem. It has happened many times in the past. It will happen in the future.

DETECTION

You can sense a problem if management is getting interested in the plan and its recommendations but is not dealing with the resource and money issues. They are seeing the problem from one perspective.

ACTIONS AND PREVENTION

When the IT planning effort is started, you want to lay out some potential scenarios for what might happen. We have used this time to emphasize the political benefits of the plan — that of controlling and redirecting resources. Another benefit is that it gives an opportunity for management to have the business units pay more attention to IT matters.

LACK OF A DEFINED BUSINESS VISION OR MISSION

DISCUSSION

Don't all businesses have mission or vision statements? Most do. However, many employees may not see how these statements apply to them. After all, they just do their detailed work.

Some companies have developed no vision or mission, for a number of reasons. The company could have recently been created or the company has changed. The existing mission or vision, which used to work, is now irrelevant. Some managers do not see the value of the mission or vision. They may deal with tangible goals.

IMPACT

The mission or vision is useful for several things. First, it can be employed to determine which are the critical business issues and processes. Thus, it helps to set priorities. A second use is to provide an umbrella for all of the disparate and diverse business units. Lack of a mission or vision means that you receive none of these benefits. More decisions may be made ad hoc.

For the IT planning effort, there is nothing to link the plan to the business. You can work your way across from IT to the business processes. Then the analysis stops. The IT plan can be attacked because of its unknown value to the business.

DETECTION

In five minutes you can determine whether there is a mission or vision statement. That is simple. Now you have to probe whether the mission or vision is still valid and is valued by management. If the statement was defined under previous management, the new present managers may not view it as especially relevant.

What do you do? You lack the luxury to spend much time on this. You can proceed to map the existing statement to some of the processes.

You can also analyze the mission or vision statement itself. A complete mission or vision should spell out the mission or vision in terms of the following perspectives:

- Shareholders
- Management
- Employees
- Processes
- Customers

Here you may uncover gaps and shortcomings. How did this happen? Often, the mission or vision is defined in off-site management meetings. There is time pressure to get this done, since it is often viewed as management overhead. Then there is the cost of the outside coordinator and all of the management. The result — get it done, and now.

ACTIONS AND PREVENTION

There are several things to address here. First, you may have to handle the gaps. Take the list of the perspectives. Find the missing parts. Write down potential elements for the mission or vision from that perspective. Then you can get this reviewed.

Do the same when there is no mission or vision. You will need this for the IT plan. This seems unjust. Why should the IT planning effort have to fill in the missing pieces? Isn't this a management job? Sure, theoretically and academically. However, you need it as part of the planning effort, so it has to be done.

This is not wasted work. First, management will often appreciate it when someone uses the mission or vision. There are not many business units working with the statement. Second, they can see the shortcomings of the old mission or vision. They can see the value of filling in the blanks.

DIFFICULTY SHOWING THE BENEFITS OF TECHNOLOGY PROJECTS IN THE PLAN

DISCUSSION

Let's suppose you have a number of action items, strategies, and objectives relating to IT infrastructure and technology. You understand these. The IT staff and supervisors understand them and see their need.

The problem here is how to convince nontechnical managers that these things are necessary. After all, the network and systems may be operating fine, nearly at 100%. You could try to educate them on IT concepts. This has been tried many times. It largely failed. Why? Because management has no interest. They may think that there are major problems in IT if things are so desperate that managers have to be involved in IT.

IMPACT

The technology projects may not be improved, since management sees no direct value to the business work. This is more likely to occur if the management is focused on the short term: make more profits; increase sales this year. They may see technology payoffs as long term.

DETECTION

You can detect this issue in IT if the individuals involved in the planning assume that the benefits of the technology projects are obvious. That is why you need to keep a business perspective on the IT planning efforts.

ACTIONS AND PREVENTION

The benefits of technology have been claimed for hundreds of years. Listeners to these claims hear them again and again. They start to really question the benefits and impacts since they did not witness them.

So how do you sell and market technology projects effectively in the plan, especially if you cannot rely on benefits? Turn to medicine: How does a doctor convince you to have an operation? You will endure pain, loss of work, cost, etc. The method is fear and intimidation. If you do not undergo the surgical procedure, you could be very sick or die. That is it. Let's use it. Take the current technology and project how it will deteriorate over time. Then show how the deterioration can affect the business processes. We have used this technique for over 20 years. It has proven to be most effective.

LIMITED OR NO RESOURCES TO DO THE PLANNING

DISCUSSION

We have worked with IT groups of three or four people. There were no additional resources for planning. It is often the same with larger IT groups. However, you can still develop the plan. Any kind of planning takes time. IT planning requires knowledge of technology, the business, and the current IT architecture, systems, and activities.

Many firms hire consultants to create the plan. Often, the plan is created, the consultant is paid, then work goes on, and the plan is shelved. IT management and staff have participated very little in the planning process. There was no commitment.

IMPACT

Some people use the lack of resources as an excuse not to construct the IT plan. Or they may try to do a rush job. Some may try to adapt a plan from their past work.

DETECTION

What is the attitude of IT management toward the IT planning effort? If they see it as a "big deal" or if it is a major challenge, then there is a problem.

ACTIONS AND PREVENTION

Start with the attitude toward planning. IT planning should not be viewed as a major project. It should not require massive, dedicated resources. In fact, examples have shown that if you have a number of dedicated planners, they can lose touch with reality. They get overly involved in competitive, industrial, and technology assessments. These may be useful, but they are not often critical.

What is a suitable approach? Treat IT planning as another limited project. This should be work in addition to other work. That will put pressure to get the IT plan completed. What is the role of consultants? As advisors, they can provide experience, guidelines, and checklists. They can prevent you from making mistakes.

How can you develop the IT plan quickly? Space does not allow a full discussion or presentation. Here are some tips garnered from doing over 60 IT plans.

   • Create candidate lists for the planning items — issues, objectives, etc.
   • Have business and IT review these. People are better at reacting to things than trying to invent planning elements on blank paper.
   • With the lists in hand, develop candidate tables that relate the planning elements. For example, the table of objectives versus issues can reveal how the objectives interact to resolve the issues. The table of issues versus action items can show that the fulfillment of the actions takes care of the issues.

This table-and-list approach can be developed incrementally. It is fairly easy to understand. Moreover, it is simpler to update than some massive text. You update the lists and then the tables.

FAILURE OF PAST PLANNING EFFORTS

DISCUSSION

We have seen this occur a number of times. The planning effort either failed or the IT plan was produced but never used or referred to. Here are some of the reasons for past failure.

   • The plan was developed by one person in isolation or by a consultant. There is no sharing of knowledge. There is no sense of ownership.
   • The plan did not detail specific action items. The IT plan is too fuzzy. No one sees the value of it.
   • The plan is too technical. Management could not understand, so IT discards it.

IMPACT

New planning efforts may be discouraged due to the past failures. If there is a new planning effort, there are no expectations. After all, no one wants to be involved and waste time and effort in another failure.

DETECTION

Look to see if there is a current plan and if it used. On the shelves of some managers may be evidence of past failed planning efforts. Did anyone try to gather reasons for the failure? Probably not. Why? Because everyone just wanted to drop the past.

ACTIONS AND PREVENTION

Several of our most challenging IT planning efforts followed failures in planning. In some instances, a lot of money was wasted. IT management may have a bad attitude toward IT planning.

How do you proceed in such circumstances? Take a low profile. Do not trumpet the benefits of the plan. Start with the approach defined in the discussion of the previous issue. Build lists and get reactions. You will not change minds, but you will probably get people interested.

A sure method of turning around the negative attitudes is to find some action items that can be implemented rapidly. These will not be projects. They can be lower-level policies or procedures. This will increase the confidence of IT in the plan. It can also assist with business managers who may have the same attitudes.

DECIDING WHETHER THE IT PLAN SHOULD BE BUSINESS DRIVEN OR IT DRIVEN

DISCUSSION

Many IT plans are IT driven. The plans that result are often overly technical. They do not relate to the business. If the plan is IT driven, it may be too detailed. There may be many relatively minor issues. Action items are very detailed. Some action items could be achieved in a few days or weeks.

IMPACT

If the plan is IT driven, then the level of detail may indicate to management that it is not strategic. It may be a plan for IT internally, but it is not a plan for how IT can support the business. The plan fails.

An IT-driven plan may turn off business managers from any significant involvement. They see the technical nature of the issues or action items and think that they do not apply to them. As an example, network failures or short-comings may be seen as unimportant if the network operation level is high. They may think, "This is technical stuff. Why should I get involved?"

DETECTION

Look at how the IT planning effort starts. If only IT people are doing the work, then you are a witness to the start of the issue. During the planning effort, more signs of the issue may surface. What is the level of detail of the issues and action items? Are the IT objectives and strategies worded in business terms, or are they technical too?

ACTIONS AND PREVENTION

The IT plan should be business focused. The overall purpose of IT is to provide support to the business and to help effect change and improvement in the business processes.

How do you implement a business focus with technical information? Take every technical issue and turn it into a business statement. For example, "Improve network reliability" could be modified to "Increase reliability of IT infrastructure for the processes." Do the same with IT objectives and strategies. For each technical action item you can add a phrase that indicates the benefits to the business work.

Isn't this just playing with words? Of course. However, remember that the IT plan is a tool for communicating between IT and the business. The choice of words is significant. It is just the same as personal relationships. You say the wrong words and it can take hours or days to recover.

BUSINESS BEING UNCLEAR ABOUT WHAT THEY WOULD GET FROM THE PLAN

DISCUSSION

This links to the issue on expectations. Instead of high expectations, managers in this issue have no idea what to expect. Why does this occur? One reason is that the past planning efforts were neither successful nor understandable. Another reason is that the managers lack direct experience or involvement in IT planning efforts and in plan reviews.

Chapter 14

Analysis

INTRODUCTION

This chapter begins with the definition of the problem or situation and runs through to the completion of requirements. As you will see, there are many problems with employing the traditional system life cycle, including the following.

- Seldom attaining the goal of 100% requirements
- The myth that there will be no changes once requirements are signed off
- The belief that users support the change
- The reliance on king and queen bees, senior users, for information

INCOMPLETE REQUIREMENTS

DISCUSSION

In the traditional method of requirements analysis, you gather information about user needs. You ask what process and IT problems they have. You ask them what they want. Sometimes, and probably often, you are met with a blank stare. Some people tell you what you want to hear so that you will leave. Then you return to your desk and write up the requirements. After it has been documented, you review it with them, make some changes, and get signoffs. A search for a software package or software design follows. Later it is discovered that there were many hidden requirements. New ones keep coming up all the time. But you did everything by the book.

What went wrong? The first problem is one of assumptions. The assumptions from the scenario in the preceding paragraph include the following.

- The users are willing and ready for change.
- The users have an idea of what they want.
- Most of the user problems can be fixed by IT and a system.

Time and time again, all three of these have proven to be false. The users have been doing the same things for years. As was stated in the first part of the book, king and queen bees are often in power. There are shadow systems in place.

So if users do not see the need for change, why would they know what they want to change? Your best source for new ideas is likely to be junior people. They have not been brainwashed into accepting things as they are. They also see the path to a better, more suitable job by embracing the change.

The third assumption that IT and systems are the hub of the user problems is also shown to be invalid many times. Users may have a number of issues, but these deal with work layout, policies, procedures, and organization. No one comes to fix these problems. So when IT shows up, they want these real needs fixed. When IT indicates that they cannot do anything about these, you can imagine how they feel and how cooperative they will be. The same thing happens when you visit a doctor who cannot treat you with anything except a bill!

IMPACT

The impact is that the requirements will change. The work will take longer, consume more resources, and probably be more complex than you estimated.

Then there are the political impacts. The IT staff and project leader do not trust the users. When the users state, "This is all of the changes," the IT staff and project leader do not believe it. The users, on the other hand, feel that they are not getting anything useful.

DETECTION

You can detect this problem right away by determining the real problems in the work and mapping those to the requirements. Where do you find the real requirements? Not from interviewing middle-level managers or supervisors. They have been removed from the work for some time. You find the truth from the people doing the work. Observe the work and talk casually with the people doing the work. Maybe you can persuade them to train you for a day or two.

ACTIONS AND PREVENTION

Earlier, a modified approach for gathering requirements was proposed. First you uncover problems in the work. Then you find the impacts of the problems. Expect many of the issues not to relate to IT or systems. Now the employees see the benefit of the change. Next, you can define a new process in terms of the work — not in terms of IT. This will give you information to estimate the benefits and define the requirements.

Even then this is insufficient. You also want to validate the requirements by relating each one to the work. This will also get more support for change.

INADEQUATE TIME TO GATHER REQUIREMENTS

DISCUSSION

There is never enough time. Why does this occur for requirements? It is because people try to collect requirements on all of the exceptions. This can take a very long time.

What do some IT staff do, knowing that they do not have the time? They may do a rush job. The results lead to the previous issue.

IMPACT

If requirements gathering is not planned and organized well, then people typically just collect requirements until time runs out. This will likely mean that they spend too much time with exceptions. Then they try to polish what they have. The results are changes later on as well as in the next steps. Depending on the requirements, the rest of the project can be sent down the wrong path. Redirecting the project later can cost a great deal.

DETECTION

You can detect this when you see how the requirements gathering and analysis were organized. Here are some questions to ask.

- How was the time allocated?
- How much time was spent with the users versus documenting the requirements?
- What effort was expended in review and validation?
- How many exceptions were identified?

- Were the shadow systems detected?
- How much time was spent in exceptions?

ACTIONS AND PREVENTION

To prevent the problem, you should first concentrate on common transactions. Another suggestion is to focus on the shadow systems. Recall that these are informal or formal systems and procedures that the users employ frequently.

What do you do about exceptions? Here are some guidelines.

- Do as few as possible. Remember that there can be many. You can never get them all.
- If you start doing the exceptions, where do you stop? Where do you draw the line?
- The exceptions are the turf of the king and queen bees. If you go after the exceptions, these individuals may think you are putting them out of business.
- If you automate a process with all of the exceptions, then where are the benefits? Some of the most significant benefits of automation come from standardization of transactions and elimination of exceptions. Elimination is not the same as replacement.

USERS LACKING KNOWLEDGE OF THEIR OWN PROCESSES

DISCUSSION

The employees have been doing the work for a long time. Little has changed. Why on earth would they not know their own business and how and why they do what they do? Here are some reasons that we have uncovered.

- The business rules were put into the system long ago. The employees do not remember what they are and take them for granted.
- Employees have received no updated training. The work has gradually deteriorated into a daily pattern.
- Some people do not think about what they do or why they do it. They just do it. It becomes automatic. Each workday is like the next.

IMPACT

If you assume that the users understand the details of their own work, you might develop requirements and an understanding of the process and work that is partial, incomplete, or biased in a particular direction. This can then lead to the two preceding issues.

DETECTION

Ask the following questions of the users. The answers should indicate whether this issue exists.

- How long have they been doing the work?
- When were they trained?
- Who do they go to for help?
- What is the most unusual work?
- What if they did the unusual work in the usual manner?
- Have the rules or procedures changed in the last year?

ACTIONS AND PREVENTION

If the current system has been installed for some time, then you can gather the business rules of the current system from the programmers and analysts in IT. Start here and it will save time later. While you are doing this, you can ask them about the users. Here are some more questions.

- How much contact do they have with these users?
- Who are the king and queen bees?
- With which users do they interface most often?
- What are some of the issues and problems they have experienced with these users?
- What do they think the users' level of knowledge is of their own work?
- What has changed over the past year in the user department?

When you visit the users, you now have more information. You are armed. In the user department, act dumb. Have them show you, not tell you, how they do their work.

USERS NOT BEING CREATIVE IN DEVELOPING SOLUTIONS

DISCUSSION

If the users have been doing the work for many years, they have accepted their condition. This means that they have learned to live with the problems.

They have probably defined work-arounds and shadow systems to deal with shortcomings of the current system supplied by IT.

Look at yourself. On an average day, do you feel creative? Not often. Do you look around for problems to solve? Not often. You and we behave in the same manner as the users. We do not actively seek problems to solve.

IMPACT

In defining requirements for a new system, you have to be somewhat creative. If the users do not supply the creativity, where do you get it? Often, it is from the IT staff themselves. The analyst comes up with potential solutions.

Now consider this from a psychological perspective. The analyst has defined the requirements and has some pride in his or her work. The analyst does not really want to be told that his or her requirements and creative solutions will not work. He or she also will not be very willing to change them, since time and effort have been invested in their development.

The impact may be that the solution is the one that came from the brain of the system analyst. The users really did not buy into it. No wonder they later resist the new approach.

DETECTION

When you go out to gather information, you can propose some minor changes. Get their reactions. You can then see their attitude toward change. Suppose that together you identify some problems and impacts. They agree with these. Now ask them how they could fix these. What would they do? The answer gives more insight into their creativity or lack of it.

ACTIONS AND PREVENTION

The safest approach is to assume that people are not going to be very creative. After you uncover the problems and impacts of the work, let some time pass. Let a week go by. This will give them time to think about the problems. They can talk among themselves. They may surprise you in a pleasant way and define some good ideas. Even if you are cynical, it is worth a try.

Sometimes you have to provide "triggers" to generate new ideas. Here are some good triggers.

• Do nothing. This will reveal the impact of deterioration. How will the problems and their effects worsen? This can help define the benefits.

- Throw money at the problems. This will show the limits of what's possible with financial means.
- Do anything but IT and systems. Change policies and procedures, etc. This will reveal some quick hits that can be done to alleviate the problems.
- Automate all of it. This will not be practical, but it shows the limits of automation. It also politically shows the employees that their jobs will not be eliminated by a new system.
- Combine quick hits and the new system.

UNCLEAR BENEFITS OF THE WORK

DISCUSSION

Fuzzy benefits have been around a long time. They have been tolerated by both users and IT. Why does this occur? IT may not want to press the benefits issue since they cannot make the benefits come true.

Politically, many users do not want to give tangible benefits. Why? Because then they might be held accountable for them. It is better to give fuzzy benefits.

This is what often happens to the magic measure of ROI (return on investment). Management makes a big deal of ROI in reviewing and approving new work. Several problems appear often. First, no one validates the ROI in the actual work. Second, no one asks how the ROI will come true. What actions and cuts will users make? Once the project is over, little interest is shown in determining whether the benefits were really achieved. Sound familiar?

IMPACT

What is the impact of fuzzy benefits? For one thing, no one is pressured into getting tangible benefits. The focus of the effort goes to putting in the system. The benefits can come later.

Then the system is completed and running. The IT people go on to other work. Management assumes this problem was solved. The users go back to doing the work. There were no tangible benefits. The users may not have altered the basic ways they do their work.

DETECTION

Look at the last few completed projects. What were the benefits? Was there an ROI calculation? What happened after the work was completed? Where is the report on the benefits and impacts? Was the ROI validated?

Actions and Prevention

In our experience, the best policy is to force benefits to be tangible. That is, every intangible benefit has to be turned into a tangible benefit. Let's give some examples.

- *Ease of use.* This is a classic one. Well, if something is easy to use, then it requires less training and less documentation, and the work can be done faster.
- *Less mundane, clerical work.* This frees up time for more challenging, complex work. The productivity of the staff should increase.
- *Online help.* If you have online help, people tend not to memorize the procedures. They rely on the online help system like a crutch. Guess what — the transactions may be slower. If the error rate is supposed to decline because of the online help, then you can get more work done.
- *Completeness.* The new system covers more functions than the old. This means that there should be fewer shadow systems and manual exceptions. Productivity should be higher.

When you force this (and we mean really insist on it), then you may encounter resistance. Individuals will say that the tangible benefits cannot be realized. Therefore, you wipe out the intangible benefits. Maybe then there are no benefits. Maybe this is good. The project should be killed, because there are no benefits.

A general guideline is to ask, "What will people do with the benefits? What will they do with more available time?" These are the key questions to answer for the benefits.

LACK OF REAL OVERALL MEASUREMENT OF THE PROCESS

Discussion

It is amazing to us that a project can be started, requirements gathered, and then the work of implementation begun. Then at the end of the work, when people want to know the real results, they cannot be obtained. Why? Because no one measured the process overall at the start.

Why did measurement not occur? Some people assume that because management approved the project and the user involvement is good, there is no need to measure the process. How wrong they are!

Impact

Without the measurement of the process, you and management may get the uneasy feeling that the project did not deliver the intended results. Even if the system is used, doubts linger.

Over time you may find that some managers begin to question the value of IT. They ask, "Where are all of these wonderful benefits?" This catches you off guard and you may get defensive.

DETECTION

Look at any project and see how the current work was measured. Was just the cost of the process considered? What else was included? Then move to installed systems. What benefits were cited?

ACTIONS AND PREVENTION

It is desirable to take a wider view of measuring any current process before change. You can use the measurements later politically if people question the benefits. Here are some of the measurements we like to collect (some of them are subjective):

- Cost of the process
- Number of people, by function
- Turnover of staff in the user department
- Issues and impacts in the work (useful later in showing that the new system solved some or all of these)
- Number of shadow systems (hopefully, the new system automated these)
- Number of exceptions (the new process should have eliminated some of these)
- Volume of work produced
- Average time to do a piece of work
- Role of king and queen bees (subjective, but hopefully reduced in the new process)
- Sharing of lessons learned by the business employees

OVERLY FORMAL AND UNSCALABLE ANALYSIS METHODS

DISCUSSION

Over the years many analysis methods have been proposed and tried out. Few stick. Why is this so? One reason is that they are heavily based on documentation. Another reason is that they do not provide the minimum information required to select a software package or do development.

IMPACT

If the methods used fit only larger projects for which there is more time and more resources, then you have a problem. The methods are not scalable downward to smaller projects. The analysts who have to deal with the small projects must improvise based on their knowledge and expertise.

The overall impact may be to weaken and lessen the use of the formal methods overall. The result can be a variety of inconsistent methods, which are more difficult to manage and review in terms of quality.

DETECTION

You can observe what people are doing from reviewing the last few projects. Look at several smaller projects first. They can tell you more about what methods are used.

Next, you can see if there is any management enforcement of methods. Are the methods strongly monitored in their use? Or are they just guidelines?

ACTIONS AND PREVENTION

This is not a book on systems analysis. So rather than discuss specific methods, we will try to provide some guidelines.

- Any method of analysis should focus attention on areas of risk. The user interface is often not one of these. However, interfaces, data conversion, business rules, and integration are more risky and have more issues.
- Any method employed should be scalable down to projects one month in duration. They should be applicable, for example, to substantial enhancements to current systems.
- There should be guidelines on how to use the methods. These should aim at cumulative improvement in the use of the methods.
- Each method should have an expert whom people can go to for assistance.
- The methods should be enforced and reviewed.

There is a message here. That is, you want to be cautious in adopting new methods. To be properly implemented, each new method has to have an accompanying infrastructure.

ORIGINAL STATED PROBLEM NOT BEING THE REAL PROBLEM

DISCUSSION

This is often the case in many areas of real life. You can go to a doctor with a problem. You state the problem. However, the doctor treats this as if it were a symptom. He or she does not accept the problem that you have stated, however clearly, as the truth. Tests and an examination follow. You may find that you thought you had problem A, but it turns out that you have B and C.

It is the same with an IT project and work. The managers hear secondhand about some problem, for example, a problem with the current payroll system. You go out to the payroll department and find that the system is working fine. What is the problem? Well, it turns out that the key executives get their payroll done manually due to the amount of money involved or the complexity. One manager did not get paid on time.

The stated problem may come from upper- or middle-level management. When you investigate the problem, you find that the real situation is far different. There is a catch-22.

- If you solve the stated problem, then the users may be upset since their real problems were not addressed.
- If you solve the real problems, then management may be unhappy. They may think you worked on the wrong problem.

Remember that you may not have the time or resources to solve both.

IMPACT

If you accept the problem as stated, then you could fall into a trap. You continue to pursue a false direction even when there are signs that you are headed the wrong way. This can waste effort and time. It can also lead to problems between the users and IT.

DETECTION

You can detect that the analysis is not doing well if you find there was no questioning of the problem in the early stages of work. You can also tell whether a problem exists if the users are not very excited about the new system. After all, they perceive no benefit from it because it does not solve their issues.

In the analysis you want to map the stated problem to the real one. Your goal through actions is to marry the two. That may satisfy everyone.

Actions and Prevention

Never accept a problem as stated. Take the initial problem as a "hunting license" to go out and find the real problems. This will give you more psychological flexibility. Give credit to management for stating the problem, since this triggered the effort.

Assume that the problems are multiple and at different levels: the management problem that you got at the start, middle-management problems, and problems in the work with the real employees doing it. These problems do not have to be consistent or linked. For example, a problem at a lower level can easily contribute to a problem at a higher level.

Let's take an example. Suppose the lighting in the workroom is dark. The paint is peeling and old. The floor is not clean. Employee morale is low. Middle management sees the problem in terms of the employees. They are decently paid, so they should not complain. Just accept things and get on with the work. Management sees lower productivity. Note in this example that you fix the problems at the bottom to fix the problem at the top.

REAL PROBLEMS BEING POLITICAL AND NOT TECHNICAL

Discussion

This often happens, more now than before. Why? Today, systems and IT are more embedded in the business processes. Business managers have their power based in these same processes.

IT staff tend to assume that because they were handed a problem, it must be a technical one. After all, if it was an organizational or political problem, it would not have been given to IT — right?

Management sometimes has a dilemma. They have only one group that does projects. The other departments do their normal work. The managers may not want to admit that the problem is political or organizational, so they move it down to IT.

Impact

If you treat a physical problem incorrectly, you could get really sick. It is the same with business problems. You can make the underlying problems worse by implementing a new IT solution.

IT may implement a solution that does not solve the real issues. There are no benefits. Efforts have been wasted.

Let's consider a real-life example. A firm wanted better management information. The management was told that an ERP would deliver this. They jumped at the solution. The massive ERP project was started. It was eventually implemented. Did management get and use the information? No. You see, that was not the problem. The problem was that management had no methods to deal with the information they already had been getting from the legacy systems.

Lesson learned: If you want better use of information, define the process for analyzing it. Then you can determine the shortcomings of the information. You are then in a better position to know if you need a new system.

DETECTION

You can detect the problem by observing how IT managers discuss and describe the projects. Do they and the staff acknowledge the political dimension at all? If not, then the problem is present.

This issue is also present if you see that the IT projects are all technical. In the real world, some projects should have ended with policy or procedural change. Others should have a mix of business change and IT. Few are exclusively IT.

ACTIONS AND PREVENTION

Projects and IT work change and improve business processes. As such, they affect the underlying power structure within and between departments. Thus, you can assume that each major IT effort will result in political change.

Go back to the project concept discussed in Part I of this book. There we discussed the benefits of having four purposes for each project:

- Technical purpose — what systems work will be done
- Business purpose — the goal of change in the work
- Cultural purpose — how people will work together better after the project
- Political purpose — the future alignment of power after the project is completed

LACK OF A REAL DOWNSIDE IF THE PROJECT IS NOT DONE

DISCUSSION

Most of us consider the benefits of a project or work. We tend to focus on the improvements. However, we often ignore the downside. What if the project is not done? This is frequently the most important question to answer.

If there are no bad impacts of not doing the project, then users will feel a lack of urgency to change. They may actively resist change, since things will not get worse. If IT managers feel the same way, they may put fewer and less qualified resources on the work.

IMPACT

In addition to the impacts of the last section, you can see that one impact is that the project may not get anywhere. Since there is no pressure to get it done, work proceeds slowly. People may be moved to other work.

Consider the Y2K effort. This was a major urgency and even involved some panic. Some businesses could not operate without modernized software. What happened? Not much. Why? Because management, IT, and users were driven by the one-time real, true urgency of the year 2000.

DETECTION

Take several projects. Read the project description. Visit some of the users and find out what is going on. What would happen if they had to continue to do the work in the same way? What would be the impacts if the project failed? If the answer to these questions is "not much," then you can see that there is little downside.

ACTIONS AND PREVENTION

To prevent the problem, for every new project idea answer these questions.

- What if we do not do the work?
- What if the work were deferred for a year?

The answers will assist you in determining urgency at the project level.

Now move up to the project slate. This is the group of potential projects that IT could work on in the next period. Rank these in different ways, including:

- ROI
- Risk
- Urgency — the pain if the project is not done
- Alignment or support of the mission or vision of the organization

You will find that the relative ranking of each project is different. Those that have a high ROI, for example, may not have high urgency. We suggest that management will likely go after the urgent projects. Why? Fear of what will happen if they do not do these. The others can wait.

CONCLUSIONS

Nowhere here have we suggested that you change whatever methods of systems analysis you are using. Rather, we have tried to add guidelines to help you avoid some of the most common pitfalls in analysis. This is important since, as you are well aware, if a project gets started on the wrong foot, it is difficult to recover.

Software Packages

INTRODUCTION

Software packages, which have been around for 40 years, have posed a dilemma in IT and the business. Should you develop software that fits your needs better and more of your requirements? Or should you buy a software package that does not do everything but gives you some capabilities with less cost and, more importantly, less risk?

Most software packages are 10–15 years old. They have been modified and upgraded through new releases a number of times. The number of major software firms has declined through mergers and acquisitions. Yet you would not think of building large complex software systems on your own. Nor would you want to construct software when there are established, less expensive alternatives. So packages will always be part of the main software of an organization. Note, however, that some firms still see software as a competitive advantage. Wal-Mart develops and maintains their own systems. However, few can match their resources.

Given that you are going to buy or already have software packages, what are some guidelines that can be gleaned from past experience? Here is a basic one:

> **It is not what you get with the software that counts;**
> **it is what you did not get that matters.**

What does this mean? No software package can meet all of your needs. Therefore, you have to compromise. Either you have to warp your processes to fit the software package or you have to invent new shadow systems or continue to use the existing software that met your needs yesterday.

NO SOFTWARE PACKAGE THAT FITS THE REQUIREMENTS

DISCUSSION

Software packages have limited flexibility. You can change table values and parameters, but you cannot change the structure of the software. In the preceding discussion, we pointed to the gap between the software and the requirements.

IMPACT

Suppose you acquire a package and think that it fits your business well. Later, you find out that this is not the reality, that a major gap exists between the package and the process. The business impact is to force unpleasant and untimely decisions about the processes and how to change them.

There is also a political impact. The users and IT probably will have less faith in management. They think that management really did not care about them or their processes; they just went out and bought something without thinking it through.

DETECTION

You can detect this problem by seeing what happened in firms in the same industry segment as yours with various packages. If they had major problems in implementation, you might as well, unless, magically, a new release solved these problems.

ACTIONS AND PREVENTION

You have several choices. You have to make a decision. Involving the users here is a good idea since they may be severely or substantially affected. Here are the options.

- Continue to run the existing system. Enhance it but do not replace it.
- Buy the software package and try to customize it as much as possible.

- Change and streamline the business process and work and then consider the software packages.

We prefer the third option. It provides the best long-term solution. Simplify the requirements for the new software package and it will fit better. Moreover, you may find that when you change and simplify the process, the current software still meets your needs.

You should not assume that buying a new software package will force the users to change. They may resist change and continue to use the same process with the new package, in which case there is likely to be few, if any, benefits.

Another possibility is that the users really try to fit into the package, but it is not a good fit. Then you have to create more shadow systems.

LACK OF VENDOR SUPPORT IN THE CLIENT LOCATION

DISCUSSION

This can be a major issue when the headquarters IT group acquires the software for distribution and installation at multiple locations in different countries. The vendor could have indicated that support was available; it turns out to be untrue. Alternatively, the headquarters IT group assumes that since the package is from a known vendor, support will be available. If the vendor does not provide direct support in some locations, then the firm may have to resort to a mixture of third-party firms for support in implementation.

The type of vendor support needed includes:

- Setup and installation of the software
- Installation of support software and utilities
- Training of the operations staff in software operations
- Training of IT and users in the implementation of the package

Here we differentiate between the direct installation of the software and the implementation. Implementation includes the customization of control tables and interfaces. At the end of installation you are ready for implementation. At the end of implementation, the system is in production with the end users.

IMPACT

This issue may not emerge until the software vendor is ready to install the system in one or more remote locations. Experience shows that this can cause major delays. There are added costs if the vendor has to fly people around the world. Another option is to find a local, in-country firm that supports the installation.

There are also political costs. The burden of dealing with a local firm falls on the IT group in that location. This group may be so small that much of their current work has to be suspended.

Installation, however, is simpler than implementation. Implementation takes time and effort because you have to find the best fit between the processes in each location and the functions and capabilities of the software package. Implementation of major packages such as ERP systems usually requires consultants. Are there local consultants that are qualified and experienced? The local IT group should be involved in their evaluation and selection. Like installation, this takes the IT group away from their normal work. If the consultants have to be flown in, then there are coordination, management, travel, and additional labor costs.

DETECTION

You will undoubtedly ask the vendor about what is available at the major company locations. Sales and marketing people will probably give you an answer you want to hear. You need to validate the answers with the local IT group.

Another step is to contact users of the software package in the various locations. Find out about vendor support. Also, uncover what consultants and third-party vendors can do. Determine how the users implemented the package, taking into account local regulations, rules, and customs.

ACTIONS AND PREVENTION

The best preventive action is to involve the local IT groups from the beginning. In addition to getting them involved in checking out vendors, they need to figure out how they can allocate resources to support the installation and implementation. Some involvement of local users is useful as well.

It is a good idea to try to streamline and standardize the processes at the different locations *before* the new software package is selected. Some people wait until the package is selected and then try to solve the differences in the processes during the implementation. This is too late. If you wait, the users will be forced simultaneously to change their processes and understand how the new system works. This is too great a burden, given that they will also have to be doing their regular work.

SOFTWARE WITH NO NEW RELEASES IN SOME TIME

Discussion

Many firms produce and distribute new releases or versions of their software packages annually or even more frequently. The new release typically incorporates some features or functionality that were added for a specific user or were strongly urged by the user group of the package. It also will likely fix some known problems with earlier versions.

A number of factors can give rise to changes in the software. Here are some examples.

- The original software did not address certain functions. The new release fills the gap.
- The new version fixes some major design flaws that have been noticed and have affected the current systems.
- There is a new user interface that makes the system simpler to use.
- The new version provides for more reporting, improved interfaces (e.g., through XML), and increased flexibility.

Impact

Now, you know that things in IT do not stay the same. The business changes. The software environment changes. An example is the move to multiple processors that share resources. This can change the price structure and cost of the software in this example.

If there is no new release or version, then either nothing has changed or there might be a problem with the vendor. Hearing no news may mean major financial problems, for example. It is not likely that the package is perfect or that nothing has changed.

If the vendor is in trouble, the worst case is that either they get sold to someone else or go out of business. In the first instance, you may be forced to move to the acquiring vendor's package. In the second, you have to drop everything and start looking for a new vendor.

Detection

Stay in touch with the vendor. Do not assume that everything is fine. Search on the Web for the latest news on the firm. Stay in touch with user groups for the software. Another step is to establish contact with several other users that are local to you.

ACTIONS AND PREVENTION

While you cannot prevent the problem, you can use the detection steps to take action. You can also track how firms and products of competing software packages are doing. If they seem to be getting greater market share than your vendor, you could have a problem.

Periodically, you should reevaluate the software packages you are using. This is like making an assessment of your car. It runs, but it is getting older. Should you trade in the vehicle or wait? It is the same with the software package. A related action is now and then to contact competing software vendors and learn about the functions and features of their latest software.

DECIDING WHETHER OR NOT TO MOVE TO A NEW RELEASE

DISCUSSION

This issue links to the previous one. However, here there is a new release. It seems to be attractive. What should you do? Should you wait? Or should you go ahead? The answer depends on the situation. A general guideline is to have a policy to address this for all software packages. The worst course of action is to have no policy. Then each time one software package has a new release, you have to improvise a method for making the decision.

IMPACT

If you adopt the new release and it has problems, there are several impacts. First, you may have to fall back to the previous release. This affects both IT and user productivity. Second, the vendor loses credibility. This creates political problems.

If you do not install the new version, then you are missing the new capabilities. Perhaps the users and/or IT had to implement work-arounds or shadow systems to deal with the lack of these capabilities in the previous versions. Thus, failure to adopt means you continue to support these things.

Another impact is that if there are problems in performance or errors in the system that are fixed in the new version, then these are unavailable to you until you install the new version. You also have to live with these problems.

The dilemma is more severe when the new version offers major new enhancements. For example, the old version of one medical system contained several different databases. User navigation between the databases was clumsy at best, which affected user productivity substantially. In this situation there was little choice but to go ahead.

DETECTION

Look at the pattern of past releases. What did other users do? What patches and fixes were provided soon after the new release? Does the vendor in the worst case move the testing to the customers so that they become guinea pigs for the new release? Can the users and IT live without the new functions?

ACTIONS AND PREVENTION

A long-standing recommendation is to wait for yet another release. Under this strategy you would always stay one release behind. This has merit if the new release has no essential new features or functionality. Here are some of the benefits.

• There is more user experience with the release.
• Enough time has elapsed for problems to be noticed.
• The vendor has time to issue patches or emergency fixes.
• You can gain from the experience and learning curve of others.

However, if there has been a major time gap between releases and the vendor has thoroughly tested the new release, then you have more confidence in the earlier adoption.

But you do not want to get too far behind. The vendor may not support older versions forever. Each new release fixes bugs and problems that surfaced in the previous production version. If these errors are severe, you may be forced to the new release. Overall, rather than ask the question "Should I adopt the new release?" it may be safer to ask "What will happen if I wait?"

LACK OF VENDOR SUPPORT FOR THE PRODUCT

DISCUSSION

Vendors are supposed to support the products they offer. However, there are degrees of support. In the situation where the product is the major source of revenue for the firm, they will make the effort to keep it up to date and to improve it. They want to retain and expand their user base. This is especially true if other vendors are offering software that does similar things.

On the other hand, the software vendor could have been acquired by someone else. The new vendor may have little interest in updating the acquired software. Then why did they buy the company? To acquire market share, to expand their customer base. Their main interest lies in migrating you and other customers to their product. Look at what happened when J.D. Edwards was acquired by PeopleSoft.

Impact

The impacts vary by the degree of support. If the vendor does not provide new versions, that is one thing. At least the software works OK. There is no immediate, urgent problem.

However, if the vendor takes too long to provide fixes for problems or their staff is unavailable to answer questions, then the impact is more severe. The impacts can be felt in operational, production failure of the software.

Detection

You should keep in regular contact with the software vendor. Go to the Web to find out news about the vendor. If they are in a cash flow crunch or sales are down, the technical staff, except for a central core of people, may be let go.

This happened with a manufacturing firm. They were happy with the software. They did not stay in touch with the vendor. Then they started to experience technical problems. They contacted the vendor help desk and were told that the problem was being worked on. It was not. The firm was shutting down. This even appeared in the technology news digests. However, the firm did not know and made no effort to find out what was going on. How did they finally find out? They tried to call the vendor and learned that the number had been disconnected.

Actions and Prevention

Some of the actions relevant here were discussed under prevention. There are other steps. Contact the help desk on a regular basis. Appoint someone in IT to be the monitor of the vendor. They now have the responsibility to report to IT management on the status of the software vendors. This can be a major issue, since the software vendors are often very thinly capitalized. They have little money or resources for research and development to either improve the product or bring out new products. It is better now with the consolidation of the major software vendors. Twenty years ago, it was more difficult. There were more vendors and they were often very small and privately held.

SOFTWARE PACKAGE VENDOR THAT WAS ACQUIRED BY ANOTHER FIRM

DISCUSSION

J.D. Edwards was acquired by PeopleSoft. PeopleSoft was then acquired by Oracle. A bigger fish swallows a smaller fish that had already swallowed but not digested an even smaller fish.

Why do acquisitions and consolidation occur? Often, it is cheaper to buy another firm than it is to develop a rival product. Moreover, there is the learning curve to enter a new software segment. Another factor is the need to expand the customer base.

IMPACT

Support for the product you purchased from the acquired firm will be supported for some time. The problem lies in the intermediate and longer term. The new vendor has no interest in continuing to upgrade the product. They want you to migrate to their software. You are unhappy with this option. You like things the way they are. However, in the end you may have no choice.

When there is no possibility of an upgrade, the number of consultants and add-on products for the software rapidly declines. These subsidiary vendors move to the software of the acquiring vendor. You are then forced into a conversion that you did not plan or budget for.

People may cast around and play the blame game. Who selected the original software? Why did we get into this position? During the software evaluation process today, you seriously have to consider the intermediate-term viability of the vendor. They may be profitable, but are they growing? A slower rate of growth can make the software vendor more prone to a takeover.

DETECTION

You want to watch the technology news. Use the Websites in Appendix C as an aid. Go to chat rooms that relate to the software. Sometimes you can get an early warning of the problem.

ACTIONS AND PREVENTION

You cannot prevent the problem. However, you can prepare yourself for the potential of change for all but software from the largest vendors. You can also warn the users of potential problems long before they occur. With the users, you can decide how long you could keep the current software without changes, enhancements, or improvements.

PROMISED FEATURES AND FUNCTIONS THAT ARE NOT THERE

DISCUSSION

This has been going on for many years and obviously extends to many different products and services. Why does this issue continue to crop up with unfailing regularity. Here are some reasons that we have uncovered in the past.

• Some marketing and salespeople do not know the project. They sell out of a brochure and improvise answers.
• They do not have to live with the promises. They pass these along to the technical people, who have to pick up the pieces.
• The incentive and commission structure encourages them to get the initial sales instead of building on a long-term relationship.
• The salespeople do not have the time, energy, or inclination to understand the business of the prospective customer.

IMPACT

At a minimum, consideration of the software package may be dropped. Catching the salesperson in a lie could kill off any hope of a deal. Another impact is that this actually happens and the vendor has a new customer. The technical people show and are confronted with the problem. They go back to management and blame the salespeople. The salespeople, in turn, blame the technical people for being inflexible. And so it goes.

Within the vendor organization, bad feelings now exist between salespeople and the technical staff. On the customer side, the managers and IT staff do not know what to believe. They now raise many concerns about the software. Implementation is delayed. Any momentum from the acquisition of the software is lost.

- It is a good idea to line up one or more consultants to step in if the person leaves.
- Another technique is to begin to have the person share knowledge. This can often best be accomplished politically through lessons learned meetings.

Could the programmer document everything? In our experience, this does not work. One of the authors was such a programmer who wanted to turn over the knowledge and leave on good terms. It took nine months of pushing the information out in order to leave. And this was with pushing. In many situations the person sees the knowledge as security and power and will not want to share it.

DEPARTURE OF A KEY PERSON

DISCUSSION

This issue seems to occur most frequently at the worst times. There is a tight project deadline, and the critical person, user or programmer, bails out.

Who is a key person? It is not just someone with special knowledge or skills. It can be someone on whom you have learned to rely because of past performance. You trust this individual and his or her work. The person's performance is predictable. Such qualities are very valuable in an uncertain world.

IMPACT

The work that the person was to do is now undone. The schedule suffers. It will take time and a learning curve for someone new to catch on and catch up.

Moreover, the departure has political ramifications. The management may feel that the work is not well managed. This is particularly true among users who are told that their system will not be delivered on time because of the loss of a key person. They may chalk it up as another case of IT's inability to neither deliver nor manage resources.

DETECTION

There are signs that a person may be intending to leave. The individual may be absent from work to go on interviews. Earlier, he or she may be showing less interest in the work, becoming more detached. The person may not want to share information as much as previously.

You can sometimes detect the problem by what coworkers say or tell you. They may indicate that a headhunter has called and reached them. And so on.

ACTIONS AND PREVENTION

You can take steps to mitigate the damage. One is that any critical person should not be given tasks that do not deliver milestones or results for weeks or a month or more. If the person leaves before this is done, there could be a major loss.

Another step is to implement joint tasks. That is, two people are assigned to critical tasks, with one in charge. This will ensure accountability. What benefit does this give the IT manager? If two people work together, you are more likely to get the status of the work. You will also find out more about attitudes of the staff members. Another benefit is that you will have some degree of backup.

DEVELOPMENT PERFORMED AD HOC WITHOUT ADEQUATE DESIGN

DISCUSSION

Improved development environments are now available. The tools themselves are improved. Design is simpler since we are often dealing with components and object libraries. Therefore, why make a big deal out of design?

Design is probably more important than before. In COBOL times, much was left to the programming side. Designs in structured diagrams, HIPO charts, etc. was sometimes used, but you had to get down to the coding level for reality. Today, we have to specify how components and modules will relate. While the goal of efficiency is somewhat replaced with effectiveness, to create effective systems means designing for flexibility and maintainability.

IMPACT

If you rush pell mell into development, experience reveals that programming sometimes has to be redone several times. You find things during the programming that cause you to rethink the development.

Beyond the additional effort and rework, there are problems from complexity. The more you redo something and make changes, the more complex the programs become. Then they are more difficult to change and enhance later. This can play havoc with the schedule.

DETECTION

How much effort is going into design? Now, it is possible to begin programming some parts of a system if the design is not yet completed. However, with too much of this, you will see the issue arising.

ACTIONS AND PREVENTION

Design is not what it was years ago. You do not have to spend as much time designing the detailed user interface, since most of these are Web based. However, you still must design and specify the details of the navigation. Business rules have to be designed. So do interfaces. Then there is the design of how the various pieces will integrate.

A good idea is to plan out the work to answer the following question: "What is the minimum amount of design work necessary?" To address this question you must give attention to the areas that have the greatest risk. Typically, these lie in the areas mentioned in the preceding paragraph. A major fault of design work in the past has been to focus on routine and easier parts of the design, with the hard parts left to the programmers. That happened years ago when we were programmers.

LACK OF EMPHASIS ON TESTING

DISCUSSION

There should be separate environments for testing, development, and production. Twenty years ago, servers cost more than hardware, so this should not be an issue. Yet it is. Witness the fact that many Web portals go into production with errors that would have been easy to find. A separate test environment supports a more structured approach to development and helps to support better configuration management practices.

Why don't people, and in particular management, pay more attention to testing? One reason is the schedule. Testing may appear to hold things up. After all, isn't the coding better? Don't we have more debugging and testing tools? Of course we do, but at lower levels, such as module and unit testing. There is still the need for testing pertaining to integration.

IMPACT

Here is a real example. A 12-year-old was accessing a Website to purchase items and was using his father's credit card. He was trying different things with discounts. He was doing testing in effect. He found a hole that you could drive a truck through. He found a way to combine three discounts to get merchandise free. He did it and ordered $1,000 worth of goods. These arrived. There was no charge. He then ordered $18,000 worth of merchandise. The same thing happened. In a chat room he then posted how to do it. Within a week the firm had received and shipped over $1.5 million in goods. They thought e-business was great — until they found that they had given the goods away.

In the Internet economy, the problem is far worse than with conventional internal software. More people access the software than ever before. There are also more goods and information on the goods to test and verify. For one Japanese computer maker this was a problem. They advertised a new notebook on their Website. Almost immediately, they received many orders. This made them curious because this was just an incremental advance model. Then they read their own Website description, maybe some for the first time. Too bad, there were a number of zeros left out of the price in yen. In essence they gave away thousands of machines.

DETECTION

Rather than look at the testing, consider management's attitude. Is there a separate testing group? Or is the only testing performed by developers? How are the testers trained, paid, and incentivized? Is there a separate test environment? Answers here can be very revealing. You can also probe the actual testing, but this is often enough for you.

ACTIONS AND PREVENTION

The separate testing environment has been mentioned. There should be separate testers — organized apart from the developers, for separation. Here is another tip from our experience: Use the children of employees to do testing of Web-based software. Give them small gifts for each problem they uncover. Assign the older kids to review the text of the Web pages, with similar incentives. Kids, we have learned, have infinite time and are sometimes more inventive in finding ways to break the system than adults.

INADEQUATE TOOLS

DISCUSSION

Each technical IT function has its own tools. Here is a sample list. These tools may be provided by the manufacturer of the hardware, network hardware, or software. Alternatively, they may be add-on products from third parties. The third-party products were originally created to fill holes in tools made available by the manufacturers. Over time, if the third-party software is successful, then the manufacturer may buy the third party or develop and sell their own competing product. So the mix of available tools changes over time due to this factor and new releases of current tools.

- Editors
- Debuggers
- Testers
- Compilers
- Network monitoring
- Network management
- Capacity planning
- Design documentation
- Program design aids

How can this be today? Aren't there enough? You can never have sufficient tools if you are a programmer or integrator. Much of the work is still labor intensive. Things are better but by no means perfect.

Everyone has a tool kit. There are good ones and bad ones. In what ways can the tools be inadequate? Here is what experience reveals.

- Several tools might work well individually, but they do not interface with each other well.
- The documentation on the basic use of a tool is not good. Too much is left unsaid.
- There are guidelines or best practices on how best to work with the tool.
- Every tool supports a method. It is possible that two different tools support different, inconsistent methods. People are forced to use the two tools because they provide value and there is nothing else on the market.
- The tool may be incomplete. That is, for some tasks you have to take additional steps. You may have to fall back on older tools.

IMPACT

As you know from working around a house, apartment, or car, if you have poor tools, it will take longer to do the work. Moreover, any of the problems listed in the previous section have an impact on work. Inadequacy can lead to additional, unplanned work. The learning curve for the tool may be so steep that it takes as much or more time to learn how to use the tool effectively as it does to do the work.

Another impact lies in frequency of use. If you employ a tool on a casual basis, then there is some learning curve each time you start to use it. This occurs

Area	Method	Tool	Guidelines	Expert	Management Expectations

Figure 16.1 Table of Methods and Tools

with more complex electronic devices you own that you work with only occasionally.

DETECTION

You should catalog the current state of methods and tools for both internal IT staff and the consultants and IT vendors you are employing. This will give you insight into the state of the support structure. Figure 16.1 presents a useful table. In it you first identify the area. You can start with the partial list provided earlier in this chapter. The tool supports a method and makes it easier to follow. In essence the tool automates and standardizes the method. This, combined with improved productivity, provides the management benefit for the method and the tool.

What happens if you have an area with either no method or tool or both? The IT staff and/or consultants improvise their approach. There is inconsistency.

There are three additional elements in the table. Whether guidelines exist in best practices should be indicated. If no guidelines are available, then there might be a problem. Everyone may be using the method and tool differently.

There should be an expert to call on for support for a method and tool. Without an expert, the IT staff who work with the method and tool can flail around trying different approaches. This can waste time.

The last element is management expectations. Since the other elements of the table are technical, you might wonder why this is here. That's because the IT staff and consultants should know what is expected of them. They can then attempt to get the best use out of the methods and tools.

ACTIONS AND PREVENTION

Start with the table in Figure 16.1. That can reveal where the gaps are. Where there is a gap, people tend to invent their own individual solutions. Try to prevent this or act on the problem by filling the gap. Experience shows that you cannot address all of these, since you are not in the tool business.

Next, you might reconsider the choice of tools. Maybe another method has a wider range of aids and tools. The other method is more widely used.

DEVELOPERS WHO DO NOT SHARE KNOWLEDGE

DISCUSSION

Another issue, lack of teamwork, is related to this and will be addressed later in this chapter. Here we focus on a problem common to IT and many other technical disciplines. Developers or engineers may have taken years to acquire their knowledge. They also have a great deal of experience. Software developers have created their own modules that perform certain functions. They use these over and over again. We did this as programmers starting with assembler and then COBOL, C, FORTRAN, Visual Basic, etc. These modules are products of your knowledge and creativity. They help you to be more productive and can give you a competitive advantage.

Given this situation and these remarks, it is not surprising to us that technical staff are now willing to share knowledge. It should not be a surprise to you either. If you share how you do things, others could do the same work.

The experience and knowledge gives an edge to senior people in many fields. That is a main justification for paying them more than junior people with the same amount of formal training. That is the same situation for teachers in seminars and classes. A senior person, such as a full professor, has more knowledge and experience than a junior one. Both can teach out of the same textbooks, but the senior professor adds value through experience and knowledge.

IMPACT

If management does not value experience and knowledge, then they cannot see the value of this in the work. They see one person as interchangeable with another. This can impact morale and drive the senior people to seek positions with firms that *do* value the expertise, knowledge, and experience.

While it is understandable and mostly acceptable that complete knowledge sharing is not possible or even desirable, there are many times when some sharing of information is needed in IT. Developers need to share information with the people who will do maintenance. If the developers do not share the knowledge, they end up supporting the software and systems in production. Why would people want to do this? They may feel insecure or threatened. If they do maintenance, then they have a long-term job.

DETECTION

Take a look at the individuals who are providing maintenance, production support, and enhancements. If they are the same ones who did the development, you have observed the issue. Another sign appears if there is a big discrepancy in the skill and knowledge levels between junior and senior IT staff. This indicates that the senior people are hoarding information. After all, knowledge is power — in this case, informal power.

ACTIONS AND PREVENTION

You cannot force people to share knowledge directly. If you attempt this, you could run into resistance. Or the senior person may share only a part of the information and withhold the critical stuff.

What can you do indirectly? First, you can implement the approach of shared tasks that was discussed earlier in the book. This can provide pressure to get the individual to open up to someone else.

A second step, also mentioned earlier, is to implement lessons learned meetings. Since they are not being singled out, they are under major political pressure to participate. It will eventually be their turn.

A third technique is to reward knowledge sharing. This is rare. Most managers reward individual performance, which does not support any wide sharing of knowledge. You can use knowledge sharing as part of the performance review process.

LACK OF IN-DEPTH REVIEW OF WORK

DISCUSSION

The most precious asset in most IT groups is not money; it is time. There is too much to do and too little time. The pressure of time carries across all IT work. One area, work reviews, can really suffer.

An IT leader may think that since the IT staff members are qualified, it is unnecessary to review their work in detail or depth. If the leader tries to do this, the individual may take offense, responding, "Don't you trust me? I said it was done." The IT leader may not be technical or have a technical background and thus may be intimidated by a technical review, fearing a loss of respect and esteem if any ignorance is revealed in the review.

IMPACT

If IT staff members see that there is no in-depth review of their work, they may be led to the false idea that management does not care about quality — just

DETECTION

Look at the layout of the IT space. Does it facilitate teamwork? Next, examine the project plans. Are most or all of the tasks assigned to only one person? If so, you have the issue. Another thing to observe is the content of meetings. If the meetings deal with administrative matters, then there is little or no teamwork.

ACTIONS AND PREVENTION

We encounter this problem most of the time when we take over an IT group to turn it around. Here are the actions we often take.

• Assign shared tasks, with one person in charge. This will ensure accountability.
• Change the physical layout of IT. Implement shared offices to encourage teamwork and knowledge sharing.
• Implement lessons learned meeting to facilitate teamwork.
• Reward teamwork as well as individual work.

DEVELOPERS WHO CANNOT AGREE ON THE DETAILS OF THE TECHNICAL APPROACH

DISCUSSION

This issue crops up in construction, auto repair, and other fields as well. Technical people come from different experiences and backgrounds. As such, they often have different views on a technical approach.

This is actually a good thing — an opportunity. It goes bad when the disagreements are not controlled and continue unabated for days or weeks. Then it is an issue.

IMPACT

One potential impact is that in the short term, work is delayed while people try to decide what to do. Often the IT managers do not get involved. The problem worsens. For technical staff, it can be very personal and nasty. What starts out as a semiacademic discussion turns into cursing and bad language.

Over the longer term, we have seen this issue grow to divide the IT staff members into warring camps. Each camp adheres to a specific philosophy. It is difficult to get things done under these conditions.

DETECTION

Sometimes you can detect the issue by listening to what people say during their breaks or in the hallway or out where people smoke. Then you can tell if the problem is growing when the discussion moves into project meetings. Another idea is to focus on a facet of the technical issue and see how strongly the staff members react. This will indicate the depth of the disagreement.

ACTIONS AND PREVENTION

You have to look at the problem from a management perspective. After you determine the source question or issue of the disagreement, you can get the following questions answered.

• What is the impact on the business and business processes of each alternative? The discussion here can force the IT staff to talk in business terms.
• What is the impact in IT on current work?
• What is the impact in IT on maintenance, enhancements, and support?
• What if we continue to do what we are doing now?
• Is there another option?

IT people sometimes have hidden agendas. They may feel that if they win on the question, they will have easier work, more informal power, etc. Some of this can be elicited as you discuss the preceding questions.

FEW GUIDELINES FOR DOING THE WORK

DISCUSSION

This issue does not pertain to requirements; rather, it is about what is to be developed. Underlying this issue is the fact that IT may be doing this for the first time. In Star Trek terms, "You are going where no one has gone before."

Isn't most IT work related to some previous or existing work? Yes, of course. This is the exception. However, as we saw in an earlier issue, it surfaces also if the IT staff treat all new work as uncharted territory.

IMPACT

This can make the project leader give very conservative estimates based on fear, not on reality and hard information. The stretched-out schedule then raises more issues later.

Another impact is that the burden of getting the project and work started falls on the shoulders of the IT leadership. If an inexperienced IT person is in charge of the work, there could be a time of paralysis. This is not good — another delay.

DETECTION

When there is any new work, we have already said that you should examine how it is similar to the past and present work. From our combined experience of over 75 years, we have learned that even radically new technology, systems, and projects still bring many similar tasks.

ACTIONS AND PREVENTION

Early on it is critical that you determine the learning curve. What will it take to become somewhat proficient and knowledgeable about the new? Notice the word *somewhat*. There is no time to learn it all. Make a list of what is important. Stick to it.

As staff members are learning it, try to force the immediate application of the knowledge. Also, so that the project is not terribly slowed down, you should initiate other, parallel work in data conversion and the like. Hold lessons learned meetings to share the information. The manager should attend these. Feel free to ask commonsense management questions so that you understand and so that individuals who do not want to appear stupid understand.

LACK OF APPLYING PAST KNOWLEDGE AND EXPERIENCE

DISCUSSION

Some IT people have been trained in school to approach each problem as new. In a class that lasts 10–16 weeks, there is little opportunity to use lessons learned from the past. Yet history tells us that this was a vital factor in the success of military campaigns as well as survival of empires. Look at ancient Rome. The technology and methods for building aqueducts improved for many years until the Romans had, in their time, perfected it. There is evidence that they gathered and used lessons learned. It has been the same with famous military commanders, such as Alexander the Great, Hannibal, Napoleon, and modern-day successful generals.

Why doesn't everyone in IT use lessons learned? One answer is culture. People may want to think that what they do is art. If it is art, then each project is unique. The work is unique. The issues and problems are unique. You might be able to reuse some knowledge of tools that will be reused again and again; but for management, analysis, etc. the work is unique. This attitude helps to prevent cumulative improvement. With this view a person tends to make the same mistakes again and again — like in the movie *Groundhog Day*.

From the perspective of some IT managers, there is pressure to get the work done. Just do it. Don't sit around and relive the past. This tends to send a clear and unmistakable message to the staff that experience is not valued.

IMPACT

The short-term impact is that you will probably just plunge in and proceed with the work. You could become so focused on the work that you do not realize that you are going through the same steps and problems as before. You could have done this in less time or avoided it all together had you applied experience.

If you do not value the past, you will not make much of an attempt to gather lessons learned from the past. If you just concentrate on the present, there will be no cumulative improvement. You will never get any better at solving issues.

DETECTION

Look at how people approach the work. Do they try to apply what they learned? Now watch what happens when they finish a phase of work. Do they gather lessons learned? If not, you have the problem.

ACTIONS AND PREVENTION

If there is no effort to apply the past knowledge, then at the start of work, people ask questions such as these:

- What is the situation?
- What is wanted?

This does not sound too bad. Now look at it from the perspective of using knowledge from past work. If you received a new piece of work and applied your experience, the questions would be more wide-ranging and deeper:

- How is the new situation like the old?
- How can I apply past knowledge to get this done faster?
- What is the underlying political agenda for the request and work? What was it in the past?

Chapter 17

Implementation

INTRODUCTION

If you look at books on systems analysis and IT, you'll find little said about implementation and maintenance. Yet these are important activities. Implementation is where the rubber meets the road, so to speak. This is an area of high risk and peril. You could do all of the previous work with good quality, follow standards, and then discover that there are new issues at the end. Users are really going to resist change since the project that was over the horizon is now in their face.

USERS WHO REFUSE TO ACCEPT RESPONSIBILITY

DISCUSSION

User managers signed off on the requirements. Users participated in testing. They were trained. Now you are asking that they accept the system and place it into use. There are a number of political reasons why they refuse to take it.

- The users have to change their process.
- They do get paid more money for this extra work.
- They have to change their exceptions.
- The king and queen bees fear they will lose power.
- The users are fearful of taking on the responsibility.

- The users have done insufficient work to define the new process. How they would employ the system most effectively has not been fully worked out.

To make things worse, the user managers may not have strongly endorsed the new system.

IMPACT

If the users do not accept responsibility, what is IT going to do? How will IT respond? Often, they react in an inappropriate way. In a few cases, they may walk away from the work. This is rare. More often, they take the position that they have done their part. Everything is completed and they move the system into production.

The impact is then likely to be that the new system is either not used at all or used in some minimal fashion as an addition to the current, old process. There are no benefits. There is additional work. Moreover, the situation in the user departments could actually be worse than before the project was even started.

DETECTION

You can detect the problem if users start to raise new questions and issues. They may advance new requirements. They indicate that they are too busy. The turnover will have to be delayed.

Here are some questions to address.

- How did users react to small changes?
- What is the level of their interest in the new system?
- What questions are users asking?

ACTIONS AND PREVENTION

Begin with anticipating and planning for this. If it does not happen, you will have something rare — a pleasant surprise. Here are some additional steps.

- Degrade the performance of the current system or stop it all together as of a certain date.
- Overlap the turnover with the shutdown of the old process.

By all means, downplay the turnover as a major event. If possible, have the users start using it in production informally. Then you can have them share with each other their experiences in using the new system. This will build confidence.

USERS BEING UNAVAILABLE TO PARTICIPATE IN THE IMPLEMENTATION

DISCUSSION

The users are obviously busy doing their normal work. They are unavailable because this normal work is receiving a higher ranking. It is a matter of priorities and politics. Upper-level user managers may want the new system. Middle-level managers hear the concerns of their employees, including the king and queen bees. They are worried that if they implement, the work will suffer. Middle-level managers want today's work done as the highest priority.

IMPACT

If the users are unavailable, then the implementation may have to be deferred. After one deferral, the users give new reasons why they cannot participate. Here are some common excuses.

- We are in the middle of year-end closing.
- The business is changing.
- Some key users are sick, have left, or are on vacation.
- Too many people are taking vacation.

All of this can demoralize IT if IT is not prepared for this. Eventually, the IT staff move on to other work. The system hangs in limbo. We call this *mid-installation paralysis*. The system is completed but not installed.

If this continues for some time, it will take great effort to restart things. Here are some of the activities.

- The data has to be reconverted.
- The IT staff has to be brought back and needs time to get familiar again with the situation.
- The users have to be worked with to calm things down.
- If there is excessive elapsed time between the training and the use of the system, additional training may be needed.

DETECTION

Talk to some of the supervisors and middle-level managers. Ask them what they hear from their people. Another tip is to establish a good working relationship with junior users. Do not emphasize this tie to any other people. Informally, contact them to find out what is going on. They can act as "moles" for you.

ACTIONS AND PREVENTION

As with every issue in this chapter, anticipate this. Plan when users will be available. Find out what is happening in the departments. Emphasize that you and they want to make the transition as smooth as possible and as easy and trouble free as possible.

When you are doing the turnover, minimize, if you can, the number of people that will be using the system in production at first. You might implement the new system and process in one location or unit. Then you can expand to others.

LAST-MINUTE REQUIREMENT CHANGES

DISCUSSION

How can these come up? You gathered requirements months ago. The users signed off. Why are they doing this now? For the bulleted reasons given with the first issue. Fear of change is a major factor. If they can add more requirements, they may delay the implementation. Then they can add more. Maybe the new system will disappear and go away.

There is another political agenda beyond the factors relating to fear. The users may see this as their last opportunity to get the new system and process more like the old one with which they are deeply familiar. The old one is a known; the new is unknown.

Of course, there could have been a communication failure. IT could have gathered requirements from individuals who were not close to the work or who wanted to get a system that implemented their own ideas. Then the requirements are real.

IMPACT

New requirements mean more IT work and a delay in implementation. However, the schedule was set and the schedules of other projects depend on the completion of this one. The impact is cascading delays across multiple projects.

Another impact is that the programmers begin to lose faith in the IT leader and the systems analysts. They ask why this happened now. Why didn't IT get the requirements right in the first place? This does not bode well for future work.

DETECTION

Earlier, we talked about changing requirements. We gave some questions that probe why the change occurs now and what it means. These questions focus on what is different, why it was not detected earlier, and the effects if these changes are not made.

ACTIONS AND PREVENTION

Head this off from the start. Circulate the changing requirements questions, and tell the users that the questions must be answered before there is any change. Next, during the project, the IT project leader should visit the users often to see if anything new has come up.

Another step is to involve as many users as possible in the work. Under this approach, users would only participate in a few activities and not in the entire project. This will help validate the requirements. It will help generate political support for the implementation.

If there are valid new requirements, see if you can address these with work-arounds. You may even temporarily establish a shadow system. Maybe the new requirement can be taken care of after implementation.

If there are last-minute requirement changes, then discuss the following questions.

- Why did this surface now?
- Can the implementation continue until these things are addressed?
- What additional requirements are there?
- How has the work changed since the requirements?

The requirement changes have to be validated in the work.

LINGERING ISSUES

DISCUSSION

We have seen no implementation that is 100%. It is like building a house. Some things will still require fixing after the new occupants have moved in. So it is more than likely that there will be lingering issues.

Here are a few examples of lingering issues.

- Additional screens or reports are needed.
- Exceptions remain to be addressed.
- Some shadow systems remain.
- New work has cropped up that has to be handled by exceptions.

The true test is to decide whether these *have to* be dealt with prior to implementation or can be done later. They have to be pretty bad and prevent the users from doing their work for this to happen. It is a question of functionality, not efficiency or effectiveness.

IMPACT

If the IT staff members have to deal with these issues before implementation, delay will result, often the cascading delay mentioned earlier. This is a major problem and creates political problems between IT and the users.

If the issues can be deferred until after implementation, there is still an impact. However, it is much less severe. IT will have to schedule additional work for the already limited resources to address these things.

DETECTION

Keep track of the issues, as was discussed in Chapters 2 and 3. In that way, you can see if some issues are not likely to be resolved. Knowing this you can plan ahead for how the users could cope without the solution and still implement the system.

ACTIONS AND PREVENTION

Follow the steps in the preceding section. Then consider lingering issues as an opportunity, not a problem. What is this? Lingering issues give IT a chance to visit the users. They can see how they are using the new system. They can observe the fit of the new process with the new system. They may discover other issues. You can also measure the process.

There is also a political advantage. The users know that you are returning. Just like a bad penny, you are not going away. So the king and queen bees are more reluctant to regress or revert the new process to the old process. That is a good thing, indeed.

RESOLVED ISSUES THAT BECOME UNRESOLVED

DISCUSSION

This is a variation of several of the preceding issues. However, it happens sufficiently often that it deserves individual attention. Here are some of the reasons why this occurs.

• The users lost out on some issues. Like a gambler who loses, they feel that they can try again. Maybe, they will have better luck.
• The solution of the issues before was not complete or created some additional problems.

IMPACT

Having to revisit issues tests the patience of the project leader. "Here we go again." If the issue is treated as a new issue, then the problems discussed earlier in this chapter happen, as do the negative impacts.

DETECTION

When any "new" issue is brought up, do not accept it as a new issue. Look, you have handled many issues during the project. It is highly likely that it is really an old issue in new clothes. So what do you do? Assume the problem is an old issue that has been recast, and treat it as such.

ACTIONS AND PREVENTION

Adhere to the issues tracking in Part I of this book. Take any "new" issue and see if you and the team can warp the issue into a version or variation of an old one. Here are some things to try.

• Who is affected by the issue? Does this match up with another, previous issue?
• If you were to decide on the issue and take actions, would these be in opposition to what has been done in the past?
• How did the issue arise? What was the "trigger factor" that raised the issue?

INCOMPLETE OR UNSUITABLE USER TRAINING

DISCUSSION

Some people want to train users completely in the new system. This is especially true with technical staff who are proud of their work. You can see the same phenomenon when you go into a professional camera store. You want a simple digital camera. The salesperson shows you several and then proceeds to go into a detailed comparison. Minutes go by. You look at your watch. You are thinking, "When is this going to end?" After all, you do not need some of these fancy features. You can fix photos on a microcomputer. You are not interested in making a short movie or recording sound. Yet the presentation goes on and on. You walk out.

That example is what can occur and has occurred with users. The training they get is focused only on the system (the camera). There is little talk about how to use the system most effectively in the process and work (for example, how you would deal with batteries for the camera).

In many situations the training people do not know the business process. They are not familiar with the user jargon. They do not know the user process. When the users ask some of the following questions, they cannot answer adequately. Instead, they go back to the new system.

- How does the system handle (insert here business transaction with jargon)?
- How is this better than (insert what the old process and system do)?
- Can you make the system do (insert an exception here with jargon)?

This is acceptable if you are learning a software tool such as word processing, which is general purpose. It is a total failure for an application system.

Are the users trying to cause problems and reject the new system? Maybe they have a hidden agenda. Maybe not. Most of the time the users are trying to take this new information they are receiving for the first time and attempting to fit it into their frame of reference.

IMPACT

The direct impact is that the training may have been wasted. However, if this issue surfaces, the impacts will then go much deeper. Here is a list of potential impacts.

- The users remain unconvinced that the new system will provide value.
- There are now questions as to whether the new system can handle the work.
- Users are confused and disoriented as to what they will do when they get the system.

As you can see, the wrong training, training that is not fitted to the users and not complete in including the process can lead to major problems. In the most severe case the project fails.

DETECTION

How is the training planned? Who will do the training? Is the training in the process or the system? These are just some of the questions you can pose to uncover this issue.

ACTIONS AND PREVENTION

The most effective training happens when users either do it or participate a great deal in it. Then the audience can associate with them. The users can employ their jargon. They can relate how the work will be done.

The training should be in the process that includes the system. The training for the system should be the minimum, the bare minimum, needed to go live. Who can determine the minimum? The users can — working through a simulation.

What is an effective training approach? Imitate the television infomercial. It is a proven method. You assume that the audience does not want to change and is satisfied with the status quo. Start the training with examples from the current process. Get the users to discuss the problems in their work and the impacts on them. You will have gotten them to admit that there are problems and that they affect the work in a bad way.

Now do some training in the new process for only the transactions that you presented earlier. Have the audience participate, if possible. Now you can have the audience do a before-and-after comparison. Then you can do the detailed training in the other common transactions and regular work. Do not get bogged down in exceptions.

USERS WHO RESIST CHANGE DURING THE IMPLEMENTATION

DISCUSSION

This is an umbrella issue under which some of the other issues in this chapter fit. As was said before, you want to anticipate and expect that there will be resistance, for all of the reasons discussed before.

IMPACT

The general effect of resistance is to slow things down when concerns are addressed. You have to ameliorate the fear factor. If you attempt to paper this over or ignore it, it will come back, most of the time with a vengeance.

DETECTION

You can detect the problem by seeing how people interact with the project leader and IT as implementation draws near. The users who do not want the change are not as open. They are more reserved and may not be friendly. They may be hostile.

ACTIONS

Involvement of more users along the way is a good idea. Another is to define the new process during requirements. This will give stability to requirements. It will also lead to answering the following questions.

- What useful things should be performed that are not being done now?
- On what tasks and activities would employees like to spend more time?

New systems often free people up from clerical work. They may not have to key data into a shadow system, since the shadow system is now part of the new system. Interfaces that were once manual or partially automated are now fully automated.

As you approach implementation, you can work with the users and their management to prepare to fulfill these new duties. This is good. Why? Isn't it more work? Yes, but they are now centered on their future job. They will be more willing to give up the old ways.

USERS WHO CONTINUE TO WORK WITH THE OLD SYSTEM

DISCUSSION

The new system and process are implemented. IT declares another success. The IT staff members are reassigned. The upper-level user managers think the same; they go about their other work. Middle management also return to what they were doing.

What happened with the users? No one is watching them except the king and queen bees and their supervisors. What could happen? The king and queen bees state that some of the work cannot be done with the new system. They need to do it with the old. They go to supervisors and say, "If you want the work done on time, we have to do it the old way for now." The supervisor caves in. This is a one-time thing, right? Wrong. It will now be the start of a pattern in which the king and queen bees try to revert the process.

The users may also still feel an attachment to the old process. They may not want to let it go. Don't you find it comfortable to wear an old piece of clothing that you have had for years? We do. It is hard to change old habits.

IMPACT

If the users start to use both the old and new processes, their effectiveness and that of department employees suffers. The benefits that were estimated and thought to have been attained begin to evaporate.

DETECTION

You can revisit the users and department and find out how the work is being done. Rather than carry out interviews, just observe. See what they do. The first time you visit, they notice you and will behave differently, so visit them several times to find the truth.

ACTIONS AND PREVENTION

A basic problem is that the life cycle ends when the system is installed. Many organizations have no provision for what to do after that. This plays right into the hands of the king and queen bees.

You should inform the employees that you and user management will be measuring the process and work on a regular basis. This gives them a heads-up that you are serious. Next, you can encourage the younger employees to talk to you. Here is a basic fact:

> **The allies of the new process and system are the younger and more junior employees, who see the change as a way to make the work more interesting.**

Some may see the new process and their participation and support as a means to get promoted and advanced. It has happened many times.

PROBLEMS WITH THE DATA DISCOVERED DURING DATA CONVERSION

DISCUSSION

Data conversion is a curse, since there can be unanticipated problems with data quality and completeness. What makes the situation worse is that data conversion may be treated as a routine part of the project. It is not. It has substantial risk.

IMPACT

If the data conversion is delayed, then the new system cannot go live. But it gets worse. Fixing the data conversion may require extensive manual entry or more programming, leading to more delays to an already tight schedule.

DETECTION

If data conversion is not treated seriously at the start and given resources and attention, then you will likely see this problem later. The earlier that you uncover data problems, the more time you have to fix them. And you prevent an unpleasant surprise later.

ACTIONS AND PREVENTION

The forward planning is one step. Another step is to actively involve the users in the data analysis. We don't mean one user; we mean several users at different levels. You want to uncover how the users work with the data. Some of the data may be hidden in shadow systems. Data elements, for example, could be calculated in spreadsheets and then entered manually into the system. What were the business rules followed to do this procedure?

USER MANAGEMENT THAT IS UNWILLING TO ENFORCE TURNOVER TO THE NEW PROCESS

DISCUSSION

This is particularly true with middle-level management. They receive a lot of heat from their employees about disruption and change. The middle-level managers then raise concerns with their superiors — more fear, and going upward in the organization.

IMPACT

If the employees sense that their management has reservations and is waffling on the turnover, their fears have been realized. Now they may reveal active and open resistance to change. Just as it is difficult to turn a large ocean vessel around, it is hard to correct a problem that spans most of the user group.

DETECTION

Talk to middle-level managers. Find out if they have any questions. Ask them what they have heard. Go to the employee level and try to uncover the individuals who have raised the problems and concerns.

ACTIONS AND PREVENTION

You want to nip this problem in the bud — early. You also want to head it off if you can. Here is what we do. Raise the issue as a potential problem earlier, before implementation, with user management. Show them some of the issues presented in this chapter. Raise their level of awareness. They and you are now better prepared to cope.

INADEQUATE USER TESTING

DISCUSSION

A funny thing happened at a major airline. A major airline manufacturer produced a new toilet for one model. They gave it to their customers to test out. The thinking was that the customer could get involved in testing. The new toilet was placed in the middle of an open floor of customer service employees. There was plumbing and partitions installed. The employees were told to test it. They were given evaluation forms.

What happened? The employees did not want to use it. However, they knew that their management would be upset if they did not fill out the forms. So they decided, as a group, to fill out the forms without any testing. While they mentioned a few problems, the toilet was a success. Management collected the forms and gave them to the manufacturer. Seeing that testing was successful, the manufacturer started to install it in operational aircraft. On one early flight a heavyset person used the facility. He flushed the toilet while seated. The suction held him to the toilet. He could not get up. He called for help. The stewardess could not do the job. About 15 passengers had to form a conga line to extract the embarrassed passenger.

This cannot apply to IT work, can it? Yes, it can and does. Users are under pressure to perform their normal work. The testing takes more time. They have no time to be trained in the testing. During the testing the users try a few things, but they uncover no major problems, which makes IT staff happy. The system goes into production, and failure occurs.

IMPACT

The worse direct impact is failure in early operation. However, less dramatic things can occur. The problems do not come up all at once. They occur one by one or in small groups over time. The users begin to lose confidence in the system. Now that the system is in production, the IT people make patches and emergency fixes. This can create more problems and errors. And so it goes.

DETECTION

Here are some useful questions.

• How early in the project did the users get to do testing?
• How were the users trained to test?
• What is user management attitude toward testing? Do they view it as important or as just more work?
• Is there a systematic approach to organizing the testing?
• How many users are involved in the testing?

ACTIONS AND PREVENTION

The earlier that testing is planned, the better. The more users who are involved, the better. You also need to give the users credit for uncovering the problems. While some programmers may see bugs being discovered as bad, this is good. Users should be given some small rewards to encourage them to break the system.

The testing by users should be done in the setting and context of the new process. Testing, except in the earliest stages, should be performed in user areas — not in IT, which is unrealistic. The more realistic the testing is, the better the results.

Use the testing by employees as a vehicle to generate operations procedures and training materials. Select some of the people in the testing to participate in testing. Have these individuals give some testimonials about how the system is now better and that problems were fixed.

CONCLUSIONS

Many of the issues in implementation had their roots, and could have been prevented, much earlier. If not prevented, at least they could have been handled more rapidly and effectively during implementation. People doing the project work may be getting tired, but when the implementation kicks off, the fun is just beginning. So are the games some people play.

Chapter 18

Operations and Support

INTRODUCTION

Much of the IT resource pool is plowed into three activities:

- Support for operations, networks, and applications
- Maintenance to fix or repair software so that it meets the original or approved requirements
- Enhancements to improve the features, capabilities, or performance of the software

What is left over is further consumed in management, supervision, and administration. Take that away and you get the resources available for projects. The survey in Appendix A shows that the percentage of resources for projects can vary widely. However, it often is around 35–45% — less than half.

This is part of the frustration that faces an IT manager. As the manager you want to do projects to improve the business processes. Yet your people are spending much of their energy and time just keeping things going. A critical success factor for an IT manager is the ability to manage and control the percentage of nonproject time.

MANY IT STAFF MEMBERS PREFERRING OPERATIONS SUPPORT TO PROJECTS

DISCUSSION

You might expect most IT staff to prefer the challenge of projects to that of routine work. In our experience, the opposite holds. Normal support and maintenance work has the following benefits to the IT staff.

- There is less pressure to get the work done.
- You might receive praise and applause from users.
- You do not have the oversight of the project leader.
- Support allows you to work with things that you know and are familiar with.
- Chances are good that you can finish the work that day, unlike a project where the work extends for weeks and months. You feel good because you accomplished something.
- You did not have to be especially creative.

These same benefits apply to plumbers and electricians who favor fixing problems rather than installing new pipe or wire.

IMPACT

The impacts of this issue are both subtle and direct. Given several tasks involving maintenance or development, the staff member may choose support. The project and development will then suffer. They will get around to it — later.

There are subtle impacts if most of the staff favors operations. IT management may find it more difficult to achieve substantial work progress on time. Management and users may sense this is true. Then they want the new projects outsourced.

DETECTION

You could talk to some of the IT and see what they like to do. Here are some questions that can unearth the issue.

- Where do you now spend most of your time?
- Has this changed much in the past year?
- On what activities would you like to spend more time?
- Where would you like to spend more time?
- What is success in your work?
- What types of things give you the greatest rewards and the most problems?

ACTIONS AND PREVENTION

It is very difficult to change fundamental attitudes. In fact, it may be impossible. Our advice: Don't even try with the senior IT staff. Their patterns are set. Concentrate on the younger staff.

Assume that many would prefer support and maintenance. What should you do? Try to make every effort to control the work in support. Most of the support work has little justification, especially when you compare it with projects. Projects need extensive justification, user support, and ROI (return on investment). Take a harder line. Get the people to address the following questions.

- What if we do not supply the support? What will happen?
- What if the activity is deferred?
- Can the resources be better applied to projects or other work?
- Can the enhancements be bundled so that the work can be performed at one time?

Here is another tip. Every week, hold a meeting with the IT managers to assign priorities for the work of key staff. You are not going to do for everyone; there is not enough time. Concentrate on the relatively few that are required for projects.

TOO MUCH EMERGENCY WORK

DISCUSSION

Emergency fixes and work is in response to a major, immediate problem. Here are some examples.

- An application hangs up or freezes.
- The network experiences a sharp slow down in response time.
- Management issues an emergency request for a specific report.
- Problems arise in the business rules for an application.
- The interface between two systems fails.
- The network fails.
- The operating system issues a major error message that cannot be immediately fixed.

This happens at your home if your plumbing breaks or if the electrical service fails. You have to drop everything and devote all of your time and energy to the crisis.

Fixing a problem is neither simple nor fast. You have to perform most of the following tasks.

- You have to see the problem for yourself.
- If the problem is sporadic, then you may have to create conditions to repeat its occurrence.
- The problem must be diagnosed. What caused the problem? This is not simple to uncover since there could be multiple causes. The components may have come from different vendors.

- You then have to find one or more potential solutions.
- Each possible solution must be evaluated and possibly tested.
- You have to make the fixes or changes.
- You must test the changes.
- The change has to be placed in production.
- You should document the approach and the change for future reference.

In the perfect world, none of this stuff would arise. In the real world, even in well-run, world-class organizations, emergencies in IT occur and recur. It is due to the complexity of what is being used.

What are some of the sources of the emergencies? It depends on the situation and architecture. Here is a list.

- The hardware and network are exceedingly complex.
- You are employing products and services from a wide variety of vendors.
- The application systems are very old. Legacy systems are sometimes difficult to fix.
- Many different people worked on the same system over time.
- There is a lack of systematic testing.
- The network management, monitoring, and security software are old.

IMPACT

One emergency could consume days, not just hours. All other work is deferred. Once the emergency passes, it takes time to get back up to speed on what you were doing before.

The impacts can be longer lasting. When someone made a fix, perhaps they did it in haste, which creates more problems. There are now more emergencies. The system or network can become unstable.

If many of the emergencies are visible to management and users, upper management may question the abilities and management of IT. They might think that other, similar organizations do not have these problems. These problems did not surface in the business units that they used to manage. This could balloon into a major political issue.

DETECTION

Consider the last month or so, and see where the IT staff spent time. How many failures occurred? How severe were these in terms of impact on business processes? Do some problems tend to recur? In other words, were they never fixed properly?

ACTIONS AND PREVENTION

No one is saying that you can prevent all emergencies. However, just like issues in other areas of IT work, you can track issues. You can observe how long it took to do the repair, whether the fix worked (no new problems occurred), and what the impacts of the failures were.

Having isolated some of the major production and operations problems, you can create small projects to cope with these on a more systematic basic.

SOME STAFF USING MAINTENANCE AS A CHANCE TO REDEVELOP SOFTWARE

DISCUSSION

You are a programmer who does maintenance on one or two key systems. You have to go in and make a change. You look at the code and find that the design is not very good. The program has run for some time and has had no problems. You are adding a new feature. The temptation is to rewrite the program to include the new feature.

IMPACT

The impact is not just more time; errors can be created because the programmer did not consider all of the ramifications of the rewrite. The code may be used by other programmers. If you rewrite it, these dependent programs and routines may fail.

In one instance the problem became so bad that another programmer had to restore the old program and make the change. That is a good reason to have adequate configuration management.

DETECTION

Most of the time, only the programmer is aware of this rewrite. Management becomes aware only when the new program has more problems or when the programming assignment takes too long.

ACTIONS AND PREVENTION

A good step is to understand your programming and operations staff. Do they like to do creative work? Do they really get a kick out of programming?

If the answers are negative, then the programmer will likely just do the change. There will be no rewrite.

You also need to manage the programming staff. Assign background and foreground tasks. Make sure they do not have the luxury of time to do this additional work. You can also emphasize to them the danger of doing a rewrite in terms of creating more errors in the code.

OVERLY COZY RELATIONSHIP BETWEEN SOME IT MANAGERS AND STAFF AND USERS

DISCUSSION

You might be thinking that the relationship between the IT group and users is a distant one. Think again. Over time the IT supervisors work with the same user supervisors and staff again and again. Social relationships, friendships, and even romance may develop.

At first glance, this seems good. They communicate well, so there will be fewer misunderstandings. Correct. However, the users may take advantage of these relationships and make some casual requests.

It goes the other way as well. The IT supervisor may tell his or her counterpart that the programmer has some time available. Do they need anything? Wow! What service!

IMPACT

The effect of this relationship is that substantial IT work and resources are consumed in work that has not been justified. This would be acceptable if there was an excess of IT resources. This is never, never the situation. IT resources are thinly spread.

In this example, suppose the IT manager needs the programmer to do some important work. The IT supervisor may tell the manager that the programmer is working on something now and the manager's request will just have to wait.

DETECTION

Here is one technique we have employed. Go to the user supervisors who have been in their positions for a long time. Ask them what they think of IT. If they say that IT is somewhat OK but is not too responsive, then there is probably no relationship.

If, however, they say that IT service is good or great and that IT is very responsive, you have to wonder what is going on. This does not fit the pattern. There probably is a relationship. Now ask who in IT they work with and interface with the most. Go back to IT and ask the same questions of the named IT supervisor.

ACTIONS AND PREVENTION

You will not have an easy time breaking the relationship and tie. Do not even try, for it could damage the relationship between IT and the entire group of users. Stress to the IT supervisors that all work requests must be reviewed and approved.

Follow this up with reviews of what the programmers are doing. Do not go to the users and tell them to stop making requests in this way. This will create bad feeling and animosity. Moreover, they will know that you are onto them. They may then do it underground.

OVERLY SPECIALIZED SUPPORT REQUIREMENTS

DISCUSSION

Harry the programmer supports system A. Mary supports system B. William works with C. We could say similar things about the hardware, system software, and network. It seems efficient and effective. If a programmer specializes in one system, he or she becomes highly knowledgeable and adept at making changes efficiently and effectively.

IMPACT

Specialization can be a curse. If one programmer is overloaded, you cannot put additional resources in to help. Meanwhile, in the next cubicle, another programmer has little to do. This is uneven use of resources.

This problem can appear to management. With all of these people in IT, why can't they get more done? Management may question the abilities of IT management to direct and control their own staff.

DETECTION

You can find this issue by mapping either the architecture or applications to the staff. Put the elements of the architecture or applications in a table as rows. Put the support staff or programmers in as columns. Place an X in the table if that person supports and has knowledge of that architecture component or application. This is a good map to create and maintain. It reveals the extent of specialization.

ACTIONS AND PREVENTION

If you started an IT group from scratch, you might be able to prevent this issue from arising by having cross-training and shared work. This is not common. You inherit a situation most often. How do you respond?

Create the table described in the previous section. Then begin to implement some shared work. Do this initially with junior people. Senior staff members may enjoy working solo. You can also achieve more knowledge sharing through lessons learned meetings. To get people to participate, you can indicate how dire the consequences could be if they were to get sick at the same time that an emergency related to their work happened.

LACK OF MEASUREMENT OF SUPPORT AND MAINTENANCE

DISCUSSION

There are many metrics for projects in IT. There are also service-level metrics for IT support in general. Much less is available for the activities related to support and maintenance at a more detailed level.

Why does this occur? Researchers and others may not be turned on to support and maintenance. Managers may think these activities are just to be endured. Hence, there are few, if any, measurements.

IMPACT

When you fail to measure something, the people doing the work become aware of this. They may behave and work accordingly. They may feel more free to spend time according to their own agenda and what they like to do. What they want to do may not fit with the overall goals and direction of IT.

DETECTION

What measurements are used in, say, program maintenance? Or are the measurements taken at the gross, total hour level? That is, how much total time did Harry spend in maintenance?

- What was the total time of the person in support, maintenance, and enhancements?
- How was the time divided among these activities?
- To what extent was the work reviewed?
- Did the work lead to more requests?
- Is there a clear line between what work is support, maintenance, and enhancement?
- Is there a change in the mix of time spent in these activities?
- What is the average time to accomplish work in each area?
- Is there a trend in the time required in each area?

Figure 18.1   Potential Measurements of Software Maintenance and Enhancement

ACTIONS AND PREVENTION

Let's take software maintenance and enhancements as an example. Figure 18.1 provides a list of potential measures. You might select a few of these as a starting point.

NO DIFFERENTIATION BETWEEN MAINTENANCE AND ENHANCEMENT

DISCUSSION

This point was raised in the previous issue. Maintenance should be work that fixes a system or restores the performance and/or capabilities of the system to its original state. On the other hand, enhancements constitute work that increases the required performance, provides new functions, supports new data elements, etc.

Why make the distinction? Why do the extra work? Here are some reasons to justify this.

- Enhancements should be able to be better controlled. More justification should be required.
- Maintenance work, if tracked separately, can tell you a lot about the state and condition of a system.
- Users will be forced to consider maintenance and enhancements separately.

IMPACT

If maintenance and enhancement are pooled together, there is a lack of control. Users can just make requests. These are all treated the same. The result can be that much of the IT work that could have been devoted to projects and made a business difference was consumed in enhancements.

DETECTION

How are user requests treated and reviewed? Is any attempt made to sort out a repair from something that will add new functions? You can also talk to the programmers. If they treat all of the work the same, they may tell management that it is maintenance to get to do it since this appears more urgent. Repairs are more significant than most enhancements. They may tell their coworkers a different story. To them much of the work represents enhancements.

ACTIONS AND PREVENTION

Take actions to differentiate between maintenance and enhancements. Create separate evaluation criteria, request forms, and review methods for each category. Begin to measure the IT work in these categories.

Once you have set the framework in place, you can start to exert more control over enhancements. Your business objective is to reduce the enhancements to free up labor for more important work. Then you can turn your focus to maintenance and work in the same direction. You may not be as successful in maintenance, but you have to keep at it.

HOW OPERATIONS AND MAINTENANCE SHOULD BE MANAGED

DISCUSSION

This is a general issue. While we have tried to provide more detailed guidelines for the preceding issues, it is here that we want to give a general approach. The problem is that you want to instill as much control and direction of these activities as you do with projects.

IMPACT

Without a more systematic management method, the work in operations, support, maintenance, and enhancement is determined ad hoc. Work is generated from each request. While you can try to control individual requests, it is more difficult. Too much of this stuff gets through as it is. IT effectiveness and the business suffer as a result.

DETECTION

The problem of a lack of an overall management method can be determined by looking at how the work is reviewed prior to the start of the work. It can also be seen in "shadow work" in which users contact IT supervisors and staff directly.

ACTIONS AND PREVENTION

All of IT should be governed as projects. You may respond, "You have to be kidding. If you did that, it might take longer to do the planning than the actual work. A bad idea." No, not really. What we are saying is that having the same consistent management approach across all of IT yields substantial benefits.

Now, with that said, how do you implement the method? Well, you can use project templates for all work in IT. Small projects have small or tiny templates of a few tasks. The IT staff members have to report on the routine, nonproject work as projects.

Next, you can gather lessons learned across all of the IT work. This will assist in approaching a key IT goal — cumulative improvement. Related to this is issues management. Support has recurring issues. So do maintenance and enhancement. If you see the same issues recurring, you can act to solve these once and maybe for all.

We have employed this method for the last four IT groups we have managed. They work. There is an effort in transition. But this is more than offset by the following benefits.

- You can do multiple project analysis across all of IT to see where the resources are going.
- You can use the information to more proactively allocate the scarce or limited IT resources.
- You can take advantage of the structure to control effort expended in nonproject work.
- Communication is better with users and management since you are speaking from a position of much more valuable and detailed information.

CONCLUSIONS

A basic point of this chapter has been that support, operations, and maintenance have to be managed as well as projects. It is best if they are managed like small projects. This is easier than you think, since IT already is geared up for projects. You have noticed in this chapter that we drew analogies to common non-IT work. This is not by accident. If you read some of the literature in construction and engineering, for example, you will find the same problems and issues.

Appendix A
The Results of a Survey on IT Issues

PURPOSE AND DESIGN OF THE SURVEY

The survey was carried out over a 1-year period. Names were gathered through seminars and mailing lists from professional societies. After the initial design of the survey, a pilot effort was conducted among 50 organizations. The results of this pilot effort were then employed to generate the final survey.

Survey respondents were provided with the survey through e-mail. If no response was received after two weeks, there were two follow-up e-mails. Each respondent was provided with the survey results. Figure A.1 gives the areas of the survey.

SURVEY FINDINGS

Space is not sufficient to present all of the analysis. The summary items selected here are those that apply to the issues presented in the book.

In total the breakdown of the responses was as follows:

- 212 completed surveys
- 21 different countries
- 30 specific industries

This represented a response rate of 64%.

The general findings were as follows:

- Project Work
  - Range — 30–75%
  - Average — 39%

Part 1: Background of Your Organization and Projects
1.1. Industry
1.2. Country
1.3. Annual sales and currency
1.4. IT budget
1.5. Number of employees
1.6. Number of IT employees
1.7. Equivalent number of consultants and contractors
1.8. Percentage of IT budget for outsourcing
1.9. Percentage of IT resources in projects, software support, general support, other
1.10. How do you determine whether some work is to be a project?
1.11. Of the total number of active projects, please indicate the mix of projects in terms of the total by duration: 3 months or less; 3–6 months; 6–9 months; 9–12 months; 12–18 months; 18–24 months; over 24 months
1.12. Of the total number of active projects, please indicate the mix of projects in terms of effort as a percentage of total projects: less than one full-time person; one person equivalent; 1–2 people; 2–3 people; 3–5 people; 5–10 people; 10–20 people; 20–50 people; over 50 people
Part 2: Your Project Management Process
2.1. What is the source of project management methodology?
2.2. How do you determine the user role in projects?
2.3. How do you determine the vendor role in projects?
2.4. How do you determine the IT role in projects?
2.5. Does your methodology have formal approaches for the following?
   • Project ideas
   • Multiple project analysis
   • WBS (work breakdown structures)
   • Project office
   • Project approval
   • Resource allocation
   • Cost/benefit analysis
   • Project reporting
   • Project reviews
   • Project documentation
   • Project termination
   • Issues management
   • Lessons learned
   • Change management
2.6. How long have you had the methodology in place?
2.7. What is the level of satisfaction with your project management methodology?
2.8. What are the greatest benefits of the methodology?
2.9. What are the greatest drawbacks of the methodology?
2.10. Are you planning on replacing the methodology?
2.11. Please indicate the source of projects (5 — very often, 1 — never)
   • User request
   • Management directive
   • Headquarters directive
   • Government requirement
   • Obsolete technology
   • IT requirements and need
   • Competitive pressure
   • Vendor opportunity
   • Strategic business plan
   • Process improvement
2.12. Please indicate how projects are approved (5 — very often, 1 — never):
   • Management decision
   • ROI analysis

Figure A.1   Contents of the Survey

- Risk analysis
- Informal process
- Management steering committee
- Urgency analysis
- Pressure from users
- Headquarters decision
- IT manager

2.13. How do you allocate resources between project and nonproject work?
2.14. Please indicate the source of your project leaders (5 — very often, 1 — never):
- Internal promotion within IT
- Hiring from user departments
- External hiring

2.15. Please indicate the project management automated tools used:
- Project management software
- Groupware
- Web-based tools
- Spreadsheets
- Other

Part 3: Project Performance
The following questions were asked for projects over the past three years.
3.1. About what percentage of the projects were completed at all?
3.2. About what percentage of the projects were completed within budget?
3.3. About what percentage of the projects were completed on time?
3.4. Of the projects completed, what percentage delivered tangible benefits?
3.5. Of the projects completed, what percentage had their benefits measured?
3.6. How would you rate the following reasons for canceling a project? (5 — main reason; 1 — not a reason)
- Inadequate project progress
- Changed requirements
- Departure of staff
- Turnover of users
- Loss of a key sponsor
- Technical problems
- Other work with higher priority
- Overly large scope of the project
- Lack of technical skills
- Change in management direction

Part 4: Project Management Issues and Areas of Improvement
4.1. Overall, please rank the following issues in terms of frequency and severity on a scale of 1–5:
- Management issues
- User department issues
- Technology issues
- Vendor issues
- Headquarters issues
- Existing systems issues
- Process issues

4.2. Please rate the following IT related issues (5 — very high, 1 — very low):
- Technology gaps
- Lack of technical expertise
- Key IT staff spread too thin
- Resistance to new methods
- Too much nonproject work
- Lack of training in new tools
- Backlog of work requests
- Changing IT priorities
- Maintenance of current systems

Figure A.1   *Continued*

- Operations support burden
- Network reliability/stability
- Test environment
- Legacy systems
- Low staff productivity
- Other — please state

4.3. Please rate the following user related issues (5 — very high, 1 — very low):
- User lack of process knowledge
- User resistance to change
- Turnover of key users
- Too many shadow systems
- Poor user training
- Users too busy to participate
- Interdepartmental conflicts
- Indecision of user management
- Weak user leadership
- Users can resist upper management
- Other — please state

4.4. Please rate the following management-related issues (5 — very high, 1 — very low):
- Excessive management expectations
- Changing management priorities
- Management turnover
- Overinvolvement by managers
- Disinterest by managers
- Poor communications with management
- Other — please state

4.5. Please rate the following vendor-related issues (5 — very high, 1 — very low):
- Vendor staff lacking skills
- Poor vendor management
- Vendor not managing project
- Poor vendor tools
- Lack of vendor experience
- Vendor overpromises
- Poor vendor performance
- Vendor staff turnover
- Poor contract
- Other — please state

4.6. Please rate the following headquarters-related issues (5 — very high, 1 — very low):
- Headquarters dictates schedules
- Headquarters specifies software
- Headquarters specifies methods
- Headquarters specifies tools
- Headquarters specifies vendors
- Other — please state

4.7. Please indicate the degree to which each of the following would improve your project management process and results (5 — very high, 1 — very low):
- New project management methods
- New project management tools
- Improved training of IT staff
- Improved training of users
- Reduced interference from management
- Reduced interference from headquarters
- Other — please state

Figure A.1 *Continued*

- Mix of projects
  - Most — 3–12 months long
  - About 30% have substantial projects over 12 months
  - Average — 9–12 months
- Number of people on a project
  - Most — 2–5 people
  - About 20% have over 5 people
  - Average — 2–3 people
- Average time of methodology — 2–3 years
- Source of project leaders–internal promotion within IT

Note that the survey included many small projects. In many past surveys, the failure rate was over 50%. This was probably due to the fact that these surveys concentrated their attention on larger and longer projects.

With respect to formal methods in place the following information was derived.

- High — over 80%
  - Formal — project approval
  - Formal — cost/benefit analysis
  - Formal — project reviews
  - Formal — project reporting
  - Formal — project documentation
- Medium — over 40%
  - Formal — issues management
  - Formal — project ideas
- Low — less than 40%
  - Formal — WBS
  - Formal — project termination
  - Formal — lessons learned
  - Formal — multiple project analysis
  - Formal — project office
  - Formal — resource allocation
  - Change management

Note that issues management, lessons learned, and change management all rank low in terms of use.

The following breakdown was obtained for the sources of the projects.

- Highest
  - Source of projects — user request
  - Source of projects — management directive
  - Source of projects — process improvement
- Medium
  - Source of projects — IT need

— Source of projects — strategic business plan
— Source of projects — government requirements
• Lowest
— Source of projects — obsolete technology
— Source of projects — competitive pressure
— Source of projects — headquarters directive
— Source of projects — vendor opportunity

It is interesting to note that most of the items in the highest and medium categories are reactive and not proactive.

The following is the frequency of the types of project approval. Note that ROI analysis is not rated highly.

• Project approval — management decision — 4
• Project approval — management steering committee — 2.8
• Project approval — ROI analysis — 2.2
• Project approval — headquarters direction — 2
• Project approval — informal process — 1.9
• Project approval — IT manager — 1.7
• Project approval — pressure from users — 1.7

The following is the average of performance statistics and reasons for cancellation of work. Note that the rate of completion is higher than in the literature (again, probably due to fact that small projects were included). Also, it is interesting to note that the rate of completion (70%) is higher than either that for being on time or that for being on budget. This probably indicates that if you are near the end of the work, you will likely push it through. Note the percentages for real and verified benefits are much lower.

• Overall completion — 70%
• Within budget — 60%
• Within schedule — 50%
• With real benefits — 30%
• Verified benefits — 35%
• Cancellation reasons
— Cancelling — change in management direction
— Cancelling — changed requirement
— Cancelling — other work has higher priority
— Cancelling — inadequate progress
— Cancelling — scope too big

The following is the ranking of issues by type. Note that management- and user-type issues dominate.

• Overall issues — management — 3.8
• Overall issues — headquarters issues — 2.9

- Overall issues — user department — 2.8
- Overall issues — process issues — 2.6
- Overall issues — technology — 2.5
- Overall issues — vendor — 2.4
- Overall issues — existing system — 2.2

Here are the ratings of IT-related issues. Look at the highest and lowest. What do they say? They indicate that adding more productivity tools for IT staff will not do much. Why? Because the staff are spread too thin. The problem is one of resource allocation. Also, note that items related to maintenance, operations, and support rank high among the issues. These activities drain resources away from projects.

- IT issues — key IT staff spread too thin — 3.3
- IT issues — maintenance — 2.8
- IT issues — legacy systems — 2.7
- IT issues — too much nonproject work — 2.7
- IT issues — operations support burden — 2.6
- IT issues — lack of training in new tools — 2.6
- IT issues — changing IT priorities — 2.5
- IT issues — technology gaps — 2.2
- IT issues — low staff productivity — 1.7

Not surprisingly, user resistance to change ranks highest. Key-user turnover, which is the loss of king and queen bees, ranks lowest.

- User issues — resistance to change — 3.5
- User issues — user management indecision — 3.0
- User issues — users too busy — 3.0
- User issues — lack process knowledge — 2.9
- User issues — interdepartmental conflicts — 2.9
- User issues — poor user training — 2.7
- User issues — users can resist upper management — 2.5
- User issues — key-user turnover — 2.2

These issues match up to the issues in the book. The highest one is for high management expectations.

- Management issues — excess management expectations — 3.4
- Management issues — changing management priorities — 3.2
- Management issues — management disinterest — 2.5
- Management issues — poor communication with management — 2.2
- Management issues — overinvolvement by management — 2.1

Here are the rankings for vendors. Only a few are significant. Also, note that the lowest is that of a poor contract.

- Vendor issues — vendor overpromises — 3.1
- Vendor issues — lack of vendor experience — 2.6
- Vendor issues — vendor does not manage work — 2.5
- Vendor issues — poor vendor management — 2.4
- Vendor issues — vendor staff turnover — 2.4
- Vendor issues — poor performance — 2.4
- Vendor issues — poor contract — 2.0

There were only two headquarters issues. Both ranked relatively low.

- Headquarters issues — headquarters dictates schedule — 2.3
- Headquarters issues — specifies vendors — 1.9

A number of improvements were proposed. Here is the ranking. Note that user training dominates the list.

- Improvement — improved training of users — 3.3
- Improvement — reduced interference from management — 2.6
- Improvement — improved training of IT staff — 2.5
- Improvement — new PM process — 2.2
- Improvement — change in vendors — 1.8

Appendix B
The Magic Cross-Reference

The Magic Cross-Reference is intended to be an easy reference for key concepts. It often serves as an alternative to the Index.

Area	Topic	Pages
Business units	Requirement changes	105–107
Business units	Requirements trade-offs	106
Change management	Resistance to change	90–93
Change management	Shadow systems	95–97
Development	Table of methods and tools	272
General approach to issues and risk management		15
IT	Differences for IT work	7–9
IT management	Alignment to the business	126–127
IT management	Key tables for analyzing current work	127
IT management	IT activities	75
IT management	Project reviews	78–79
IT planning	Checklist for IT planning and plan effectiveness	125
Methods and tools	Guidelines	74
New technology	Technology learning curve	199
New technology	Technology adoption	202
New technology	Range of potential solutions	208
Outsourcing	Vendor relationships	165–168
Processes	Shadow systems	6
Processes	King and queen bees	5, 6
Processes	Exceptions	5
Processes	Process deterioration	6
Project issues	Project and nonproject work	141
Project management	Management critical path	35
Project management	Multiple project analysis	39
Project management	Earned risk	41

Area	Topic	Pages
Project management	Open issues over time	43
Project management	Aging of open issues	43–44
Project management	Performance measures on work and projects	48
Project management	Issues analysis	28
Requirements analysis	Incomplete requirements	233–234
Requirements analysis	Four purposes of projects	245
Software packages	Selection	249
Software packages	Software releases	253–255

Appendix C
Websites

PROJECT MANAGEMENT

- Pmboulevard.com
- Gantthead.com
- Projectmanagement.ittoolbox.com
- Pmi.org — Project Management Institute site

CHANGE MANAGEMENT

- Turnaround.org — Turnaround Management Association
- Cmassociation.org — Change Management Association

TECHNOLOGY AND IT

- Baseline.com
- Bitpipeknowledge.com
- Cio.com
- Cnet.com
- Computerworld.com
- Informationweek.com
- On-linemagazine.com
- Pcworld.com
- Technologyevaluation.com
- Techrepublic.com
- Zdnet.com

Bibliography

Selected Books

Bridges, W., *Managing Transitions*, 2nd ed., Cambridge, Mass.: Perseus Books, 2003.

Phillips, J., *IT Project Management*, 2nd ed., Emeryville, Calif.: McGraw-Hill/ Osborne, 2004.

Project Management Institute, *A Guide to the Project Management Book of Knowledge (PMBOK)*, 3rd ed., Newtown Square, Penn.: Project Management Institute, 2004.

Schiesser, R., *IT Systems Management*, Englewood Cliffs, N.J.: Prentice-Hall, 2001.

Thompson, R.L. and W. Cats-Baril, *Information Technology and Management*, 2nd ed., New York: McGraw-Hill, 2002.

Wysocki, R.K. and R. McGary, *Effective Project Management*, 3rd ed., Indianapolis, Ind.: Wiley, 2003.

Books Involving the Authors

Lientz, B.P. and L. Larssen, *Manage IT as a Business*, Boston, Mass.: Elsevier Inc., 2005.

Lientz, B.P. and K.P. Rea, *Achieve Lasting Process Improvement*, Boston, Mass.: Elsevier, 2003.

Lientz, B.P. and K.P. Rea, *Breakthrough IT Change Management*, Boston, Mass.: Elsevier, 2004.

Lientz, B.P. and K.P. Rea, *Breakthrough Technology Project Management*, 2nd ed., Burlington, Mass.: Elsevier, 2002.

Lientz, B.P. and K.P. Rea, *International Project Management*, Boston, Mass.: Elsevier, 2003.

Lientz, B.P. and K.P. Rea, *Project Management for the 21st Century*, 3rd ed., Burlington, Mass.: Elsevier Publishing, 2002.

Lientz, B.P. and E.B. Swanson, *Software Maintenance Management*, Reading, Mass.: Addison-Wesley Publishing, 1980.

Index

Action items, 218
Actions on issues, 12
Ad hoc development, 268–269
Adaptation of new technology, 202
Age of the oldest outstanding major issue, 39–40
Aging of open issues, 43–44
Alignment, 13
Alignment of IT to the business, 126–127
AMD, 207
Analysis, 233ff
Analysis of risk, 33ff
ANSI, 211
Average time to resolve issues, 44–45
Average time using a project management methodology, 315

Backlog of work, 229
Balanced score card, 80
Baseline.com, 321
Benefits of the IT plan, 123
Bitpipeknowledge.com, 321
Breakthrough technology, 206
Bridges, W., 323
Business being unclear about what they would get from the plan, 228–229
Business change, 8–9
Business processes that have too many exceptions, 94–95
Business purpose of projects, 245
Business unit, 7
Business unit issues and risks, 89ff

C#, 273
Capacity planning, 75
Cats-Baril, W., 323
Challenge in turning action items in the plan into actions, 229–230
Change in vendors, 318
Change management, 14, 315
Change that does not fit our work, 147–148
Change that is too risky, 159–160
Change that means more work for the same compensation, 152–153
Changing management priorities, 317
Changing requirements, 4, 316
Checklist for IT planning and effectiveness, 125
Cio.com, 321
Cmaassociation.org, 321
Cnet.com, 321
COBOL, 60, 73, 268, 273, 283
Collaboration, 15
Common problems in issues management, 12
Compartmentalization within IT, 17
Competitive pressure, 316
Compilers, 271
Computer Associates, 196
Computerworld.com, 321
Concentration, 7
Constraints, 218
Consultant issues, 165ff
Cost and risk over time, 8
Cost–benefit analysis, 315